I've Found a Home

Teens Write About Foster Homes

By Youth Communication

Edited by Al Desetta

True Stories by Teens

I've Found a Home

EXECUTIVE EDITORS
Keith Hefner and Laura Longhine

CONTRIBUTING EDITORS
Nora McCarthy, Rachel Blustain, Sheila Feeney, Jennifer Chauhan,
Kendra Hurley, Laura Longhine, Autumn Spanne, and Hope Vanderberg

LAYOUT & DESIGN
Efrain Reyes, Jr. and Jeff Faerber

COVER ART
Elizabeth Deegan

ISBN 978-1-935552-19-2

Second, Expanded Edition

Printed in the United States of America

Youth Communication ®
New York, New York
www.youthcomm.org

Table of Contents

Contents

Contents

Contents

Introduction

Many teens feel misunderstood by their families, but adolescents living in foster homes face particularly difficult emotional challenges. Teens who have experienced abuse or neglect, or who've been moved from home to home, may find it difficult to trust. That can make adjusting to new foster parents a complicated, disorienting experience, on both sides.

I've Found a Home collects 19 true stories by teens, who write about overcoming fears, resolving conflicts, and improving communication in foster homes. Many describe forming strong bonds with foster parents, while others find a way to get out of abusive or uncaring homes. Their stories provide valuable insights on how to make foster homes work better for teens and families.

Juelz Long, author of "Deciding My Own Worth," relates an all-too-familiar experience: At age 14, he finds himself on his way to "yet another" foster home, with all the usual bad feelings roaming inside him. Will he meet the family's standards? What will go wrong this time?

Fortunately, his new placement defies his expectations. "My new foster family made me feel like I was part of the family from the day I arrived," Juelz writes. "They joked around with me, let me talk on the phone or make myself something to eat. They told me to call them Mom and Dad instead of Mrs. and Mr. Long."

Gradually, he bonds with his foster parents, who eventually adopt him.

But as other stories show, painful reminders of the past often make it harder for teens to adapt to new foster families. For Hattie Rice, adjusting to her foster mother Diane involves the slow and uncomfortable process of getting rid of emotional baggage.

"Looking back, I think some of my anger toward Diane was just my feelings about my mom spilling out, because I've never confronted my family with how they made me feel down and depressed," Hattie writes. "Instead, I tried to ignore my feelings.

But when I confronted Diane, I was probably taking all the anger of my childhood out on her."

When foster parents are patient, understanding, and respectful they can overcome these obstacles. Omar Sharif's foster mother, Ms. Bradley, shows him care and concern and encourages him to talk openly to her, but doesn't pressure him. Having been abandoned by her own mother, she understands his anger and his initial reluctance to accept her as a parent. Her approach works.

"Once I sensed Ms. Bradley loved me, I began to trust her," Omar writes. "I started to open up. I wasn't afraid of getting hurt by her because now I felt comfortable. As the first year went by, I slowly began to accept her."

In "My Foster Mom Is Mad Cool," Monique Martin explains how she began to trust her foster mom because of the way she handled conflict.

"Ms. Yvonne didn't handle the fact that I was being anti-social by screaming at me," Monique writes, "nor did she play me in front of everybody. She actually took the time to ask me what I was feeling. It felt really good to know that someone actually took the time to ask me, in a positive way, what was bothering me."

When foster parents show that they care and are trustworthy, teens are often willing to take the risk of getting attached. But adjusting to any new family is difficult. In "How to Get to Know a New Family," a therapist offers some tips to teens on how to connect with a new family, and how to know if the placement is not right for you.

Too many foster youth cycle through numerous homes and face many bad experiences. But with effort and understanding on the part of both teens and parents, foster homes can be a place of love and support. These stories show how.

In the following stories, names have been changed: Deciding My Own Worth, Not What a Foster Parent Should Be, and Rewriting the Script.

Margaret Budziar

Deciding My Own Worth

By Juelz Long

I was 14, on my way to yet another foster home with all my usual bad feelings roaming inside me. "What if I don't meet the family's standards?" I kept asking myself. "What are they going to say to me? What if I can't answer any of their questions?" I hated answering questions about myself because my answers were always negative.

As we got closer to my new home, I tried to imagine what the new family would be like. I was expecting a tired old foster mom like the ones I'd had in the past—the ones who just sat in the living room watching soap operas.

I'd lived with my cousin until I was 9 because my mother was too ill to take care of me. Then I went into foster care because my cousin wasn't taking good care of me, and she and my mom didn't get along. Since then I'd been in three foster homes. I felt like the reason people kept giving me up was because nobody liked me.

My first foster mom, Ms. Johnson, was always telling people how poorly I was doing in school, how lazy I was, and how I'd never amount to anything. She had terrible mood swings and yelled at me for everything and anything I did. It was hard for me to function around her because I knew if I made a mistake, she'd yell.

During my first summer with her, Ms. Johnson took me to my cousin's barbecue. I was excited because I hadn't been able to spend much time with my aunt and cousins since I'd gone into foster care. A friend of the family was downstairs waiting for us and I rushed out of the house.

I don't remember what I did that ticked off Ms. Johnson, but when we got downstairs I ran in front of her to get to the car and she just went off. "Boy, I am so sick and tired of you. I want you out of my house!"

She yelled so loudly that people looked out their windows. With everyone staring at me, I felt like we were on a movie set and I'd forgotten my lines. I just stood there quietly, too embarrassed and nervous to say anything.

I remember how the social worker would visit to see how things were going. When she'd ask me, "How's school?" my answer was always, "Not too good. I'm really disgusted with my performance in school and I know I could do better."

But I didn't know I could do better. I was just saying that because I was so used to Ms. Johnson saying it. She'd told me so often how disgusted she was with me that I'd become disgusted with myself. I felt my life was nothing to be proud of, nothing to talk about. My self-esteem was as low as it could be.

Now here I was again, on my way to another new home. I'd been told I'd have two new foster sisters and a foster brother, so I was expecting a bad little 6- or 7-year-old who would get on my nerves. And I wasn't expecting a father at all, since I'd never had one in any of my last three foster homes. I figured the home would be quiet and boring like the ones I was used to. Boy, was I wrong.

My new foster mother greeted me at the door and I was surprised at how young she was—probably in her early 40s. And her biological son, Solomon, was two years older than me. He showed me my new room, which was cool, with posters, a computer, and a video game system.

He told me a little about the house rules and chores, and I began to feel more relaxed. It was the first time I actually felt comfortable coming into a new foster home. Then Solomon looked out the window and said, "Daddy's home."

I felt my heart stop for a minute. I took a huge breath and tried to remain calm. I was scared that I wouldn't make a good impression. I didn't want him to think I was a big screw-up.

My new foster parents constantly told me I was smart and just as good as anyone else.

But when Mr. Long came upstairs, he just looked in the room and said, "Hello." He looked like a young, built guy. But he was more calm than scary. He didn't bother me, ask me questions, or give me a huge lecture about the rules of the house. He just walked into his room and started watching TV.

My new foster family made me feel like I was part of the family from the day I arrived. They joked around with me, let me talk on the phone or make myself something to eat. They told me to call them Mom and Dad instead of Mrs. and Mr. Long. And whenever someone asked them who I was, they'd say "my son" or "my brother."

Even so, for a while I pretty much stayed to myself. I still didn't believe I could hold a mature conversation, or any conversation at all. I didn't want to participate in any family activities, like singing in the church choir, because I was afraid I'd embarrass myself. Not because I thought I would make a mistake, but because I thought I was a mistake.

My new foster parents constantly told me I was smart, that I was just as good as anyone else and could be anything I wanted to be. They said that as long as I tried my best, I would get the best in return. I wanted to believe them, but after being told I was worthless for so long it was hard.

One day, a few weeks after I arrived, my father told me to go outside and mow the front lawn. I couldn't believe this man actually trusted me to cut his beautiful grass. I was terrified.

Solomon showed me how to turn the lawn mower on and off, and the rest was up to me. I started mowing, but stopped every two minutes because I really thought I was going to mess up. It took me about an hour to finish and when I was done it looked a little uneven. I felt I could've done better.

Sometimes I still ask myself, "Do I really belong here?" It's like I'm unsure whether I can make it last.

Even though it was my first time mowing a lawn, I didn't bother to reward myself with a pat on the back. I was just disappointed, because that was my natural response to everything I did.

I could feel the blood rushing through my body as I walked toward my dad's bedroom to tell him I'd finished. He went outside to take a look and five minutes passed before he came back inside. I heard the door close and he told me to come downstairs.

"Oh, here we go," I said to myself. I knew he was going to tell me I'd done a bad job. When I got to the last step, I was so nervous I felt like I was standing in front of millions of people.

"Pass me my bag," he said. I noticed he didn't look angry at all. But I was still waiting for him to say those five words I'd heard all my life: "You could have done better."

I gave him his bag without taking my eyes off him. Finally I couldn't wait anymore. "That was my first time cutting grass," I said. "I know I could've done much better."

Then he said something that I'd never heard before. "Well, I think you did a wonderful job. It looks real nice." Then he took

$20 out of his bag and handed it to me.

My dad didn't seem at all surprised by my success with the lawn. That's when I realized he'd already known I could do it. He believed in me.

It took somebody else's confidence in me to help me gain confidence in myself. All my life I'd accepted what people said and thought about me. Not for a second had I thought to myself, "You know what? I'm going to prove them all wrong."

Now I felt like a different person because I had different people around me. I finally had a brother I could bond with about guy things like cars and girls. I had a younger sister I could look out for and an older sister at Yale University.

I had a father who was an elementary school principal and a leader in his church. He could show me the way to manhood, teaching me how to do things like mow the lawn and paint the house so one day I'd be able to take care of my own family.

And I had a mother I could talk to. She's a junior high school guidance counselor, and when times got hard or stressful for me she was easy to confide in.

My new family fell in love with me and vice versa. After just three weeks in my new home, I decided I wanted to make things permanent. I wanted to be adopted. It took a few years to get through all the paperwork, but a week before my 17th birthday I was finally officially adopted. That was a birthday present I'll never forget.

I've been with my family for three years now, and they're like my special basketball team. In basketball, the player holding the ball has teammates to help him score the basket. My parents and siblings are my teammates and I know they'll stand behind me all the way, helping me to achieve my goals, reminding me that I can do it, that I'm worth something.

Sometimes I still find myself caught up in my emotions and asking myself, "Do I really belong here? Am I comfortable? Did I really want to be adopted?"

It's like I'm unsure whether I can make it last. I'm still working on getting that father and son connection I've never had before. There's so much to learn about being part of a family, and sometimes I'm afraid I can't learn it all.

But I guess that's what being a family is all about—ups and downs. And when I remember all the things I went through before I met my family, the things they've done to show me the light at the end of the tunnel mean even more to me.

About a month ago it was Youth Day at my church, and my mother, who's the youth president, had all the kids do an assignment. We had to take something you'd find in a building, like stairs, elevators, windows, etc., and explain it spiritually to the congregation.

I chose the incinerator, which was kind of scary because nothing in the Bible refers to an incinerator. But when it was time for me to give my speech, I was ready.

"Now we'll have 'Incinerator,' by brother Joey," my mother said. I got up and all eyes were on me. I was nervous, as usual, but for some reason I knew I had everything under control.

"That boy don't even have it written on paper! Go ahead Joe!" my father yelled out from the congregation. By the time I got to the front I had a smile on my face.

"The incinerator," I said. "This is like a dumpsite or trash can, correct?"

"Amen," replied a lady in the congregation.

"And what do we do with garbage?" I asked.

"Put it in the incinerator!" the congregation shouted back.

"You see, church," I continued, gaining more confidence as I preached on, "the garbage can be anything. It can be the stress in your life. It can be the words of people who badmouth you behind your back. What do we call those people?"

"Phonies!" the congregation replied.

With my father and now the whole church rooting me on, I figured out what it was I wanted to say. "Phonies put out negativity that we don't want around us," I said. "They only put obstacles in our way. It's up to us to say, 'I don't need that negative stuff in my life. I'm going to get rid of it and start over.' So, in reference to the incinerator, when you have garbage, get rid of it."

After I finished, many congregants made comments like, "That was beautiful," and "We have Reverend Joey in the house." I held my hand on my chest, took a deep breath, and thought, "Wow, I can't believe I did it." I'd never before let people see the bright side of me. I always got too scared, so I never accomplished anything.

That day was the start of movement for me. It made me realize that I'm smart, creative, and just as good as anybody else.

I've thrown the negative away, just like garbage. Instead, I'm taking what's useful and positive from outside myself, like the encouragement of my family, to create my own positive self-image.

Juelz was 17 when he wrote this story.

Justin Riley

Sista on the Run (From the Past)

By Wunika Hicks

I was getting ready to cook one Friday night when I asked my foster mother, Ms. Roberts, a question about dinner. She didn't hear me and asked me to repeat myself, but when I did she still didn't hear me. It seemed like I had to repeat my question 20 times before my foster mother finally heard what I said.

I was very annoyed, and as I walked out of her room I said, in a sensible tone, "Man, you act as if I'm speaking an alien language."

(Would you believe she didn't hear that, either?)

Ms. Robert's daughter heard what I said and told her mother, and then Ms. Roberts called out after me, "Wunika, what did you say?" I guess she wanted to see if I'd say the same thing again, so I walked back into her room and repeated myself. When I did,

Ms. Roberts slapped me right across the face.

The moment she slapped me I went racing for the front door. Ms. Roberts yelled after me, "Wunika, come back, come back!" but I didn't look back. I ran right into the street and kept running until I ran out of breath. I just wanted to disappear.

I ran out of the house so fast I didn't take my jacket. It was raining, but not even that could make me turn around. I wanted to call my friends. I wanted to get the heck out of my neighborhood. But I had no money or my phone book, so I sat down on the sidewalk in the rain to think of my next move.

I couldn't believe Ms. Roberts slapped me. Is that how adults express themselves when something goes wrong? (And they say we don't act our age.)

Then I realized that a couple of houses down from where I was sitting was my friend Nate's house. I remembered talking on the phone to Nate's mother, Mrs. White, about two weeks before.

I want my foster mother to know about my past, but I don't want anyone feeling sorry for me.

Mrs. White was so interested in me and asked me so many questions. She was happy I was friends with Nate and said I would be a good influence on him because she liked my attitude. I'd never had that kind of conversation with an adult before. Most times when I talk with an adult it never seems real, but Mrs. White was so open and honest. I'd never met a lady so warmhearted, someone who honestly cared about me.

I got up off the sidewalk, rang the doorbell, and Nate's brother Chris greeted me with a smile. I asked him, "Is Mrs. White home?"

Chris took me to his mother and she welcomed me with open arms, saying, "So you're Wunika!" (It was the first time we actually met face-to-face.) I was able to crack a smile because this lady lifted my spirits completely.

I told her I had run away from home because my mother slapped me. I didn't say "foster mother." It seemed so difficult to tell Mrs. White I was in foster care. I didn't want her to think I was a "troubled child."

She looked at me and said, "Your mother hasn't ever hit you before?"

Then I told her it was my foster mother who hit me, and Mrs. White shook her head as if she immediately understood.

She realized why I didn't think I had done anything wrong. On the other hand, Mrs. White could also understand where my foster mother was coming from. Ms. Roberts may have been under stress, she said, and couldn't handle me talking to her in that way. I just listened to Mrs. White explain what a mother goes through.

I tried to look at both sides of the story but I still felt my foster mother was wrong. Ms. Roberts felt that I spoke to her disrespectfully, as if she was one of my friends, but even if I had, did that make it right for her to slap me?

Ms. Roberts doesn't know that she sometimes makes me feel like my biological mother used to make me feel—like I can't do anything right.

My biological mother used to beat me for no reason, just because she was angry. She told me to keep the bruises on my body a secret from everyone, but if she was in a good mood she'd be very nice to me and say, "I'll be there for you."

My mother hurt me and made me not trust her. How can you claim to love someone and then hurt them every chance you get—physically and mentally?

My foster mother doesn't know about my past. She doesn't know that everything I once had has been taken away from me. My brother has been adopted and I haven't seen him in years. Maybe he wouldn't have been adopted if I could have shown him I loved him.

My mother abused me and I take some of the blame. I just wish I could have been a better child. My relatives didn't take me into their home when my mother couldn't take care of me. Maybe if I wasn't such a "terror," they would have accepted me.

Even my virginity has been taken away. I was raped by an older boy when I was 6.

This is a past my foster mother doesn't know. She doesn't know that I feel as if I have nothing. She doesn't know I have been abused. Perhaps if Ms. Roberts knew my past, she wouldn't have slapped me. When she did, it was like my mother slapping me all over again.

My foster mother is a decent person. I have more things than many foster children. Yet I still feel as if something is missing. There's an empty spot, a void somewhere.

I've lived with Ms. Roberts for four years now and she has never asked me about my past. She says, "You can always come to talk to me," but a child has to truly feel that and for me it's not there.

I need that mother figure—that is the void in my life.

I feel divided. I want her to know my past, but I don't want her to judge it, to say "how terrible" it was. I don't want her to ignore it, but I don't want any extra attention. I don't want to feel awkward and I don't want anyone feeling sorry for me.

And I don't want people giving me advice when they haven't been through what I have. They're just on the outside, looking in. I want to understand myself first before I let someone else try.

Perhaps I will someday find help from someone who has been through what I've been through and who's found the answers. But until then I need to do this on my own. I was the one who suffered alone. Let me recover that way, too.

Mrs. White phoned Ms. Roberts because she didn't want her to worry. When Ms. Roberts came to pick me up, Mrs. White explained my feelings of anger. My foster mother replied that I'm the child and she's the adult, and that I should speak to her with respect. She felt I had disrespected her.

I thought what Ms. Roberts was saying was one-sided, but I didn't want to say anything because I knew it wouldn't be polite. So I just kept quiet and ignored her.

When it was time to leave I gave Mrs. White a big hug as the tears just came rolling down my face. I didn't want to let go, I just wanted to stay attached to her forever. We did finally part.

I'll never forget what she told me as we were about to leave: "Wunika, I'm going to be your second mother." Those words felt so good. I melted all over.

I need that mother figure—that is the void in my life. I didn't have a bond with my biological mother, I didn't have one with my first foster mother, and I don't have one now with my second foster mother.

Don't get me wrong—I believe in God. He has done a lot of things for me and I promise to always praise Him. But I need that earthly mother and I'm just lucky I've found her.

Not much has changed in my foster home since the night Ms. Roberts slapped me, but ever since our "little incident" she seems to know my limits and vice versa. I will remember what she told me: "Wunika, you can't say everything that comes to mind."

But I also want to be able to express my feelings. My biological mother never let me do that. She would say, "A child should stay in a child's place." I can't remember ever having a decent conversation with my mother—I was too scared she'd think I was coming out of that "place."

Nothing will ever change the way I feel about my past. It's a part of my life, it affects me every day, and it will never be forgotten. You can never run away from the past. I will eventually grow stronger from it, but it has already given me strength right now.

Since the night my foster mother slapped me, I speak out to her when things aren't going right. I'm in touch with how I feel, with how I should be treated.

If anyone takes advantage of me, if anyone talks to me or treats me unfairly, I will let that person know, regardless of who they are. I will say what I have to say with respect. I will watch what I say and how I say it. But it will be said.

Wunika was 17 when she wrote this story. She now lives in California with her two children.

Nick Faxton

My Foster Mother Is My Best Friend

By Omar Sharif

My foster mother, Ms. Bradley, taught me more than my own blood mother. Through her I learned how to cope with my emotions and how to deal with life. I think it was God's intention for me to live with her and have a learning experience that stays with me to this day.

I moved in with Ms. Bradley a couple of days before my 13th birthday. Previously, I had been living with my aunt and uncle, and before that I had spent three years in a group home.

My agency felt that my aunt and uncle couldn't provide me with a stable family situation and said that it would be a good idea for me to live with a foster family. I wasn't too pleased about that because I wanted to stay with my aunt and uncle, but I didn't have any choice in the matter.

When I first moved in with Ms. Bradley I couldn't accept her as my foster mother. I didn't want to let another woman come into my life and pretend to be my mother. As far as I was concerned my aunt was my mother, because my real mother had abandoned me when I was 2 months old and I'd only seen her twice since I was born.

So I entered Ms. Bradley's house with very low self-esteem. I was a lost person. I had been bounced around from my family to the system and back again many times. I couldn't admit my anger to anyone because I didn't think that anyone could understand. But Ms. Bradley understood.

There was another foster child living with us named Matthew. Every morning after Matthew and I got dressed and ate breakfast, Ms. Bradley made us stand in front of the mirror in our bedroom and say out loud that we loved ourselves. Then she made us give ourselves a pat on the back and hug ourselves.

Once I sensed that Ms. Bradley loved me, I began to trust her.

Matthew thought Ms. Bradley was nuts. He had enough on his mind to be bothered with hugging himself and patting himself on the back. He used to get in trouble every morning because he would have a very nasty attitude about it, and Ms. Bradley would always make him do it over.

Me, I was good. I thought the whole thing was silly, but I couldn't see getting in trouble because I didn't hug myself.

It sounds funny, but each morning I went off to school in a good mood and came home in a good mood. After a couple of weeks I came to understand what Ms. Bradley was doing. She was teaching us how to love ourselves, how to build our self-confidence. I began to feel better about myself.

She helped improve our self-esteem in other ways. For example, whenever Matthew and I said, "I think I can" (which we used to say often), Ms. Bradley corrected us and made us say, "I know I can." She wanted us to have faith in ourselves. It feels better to "know" you can do something rather than "think" you can do something.

I felt loved by the way she hugged me and showed concern for my well-being. She took care of me as if I was her own. I didn't have the sense that I was taking up space in Ms. Bradley's house.

When I lived with my aunt and uncle I had every material thing, but I didn't have real love. My aunt and uncle couldn't relate to my pain because they didn't want to take the time to understand and help me. But Ms. Bradley's love was genuine.

Once I sensed that Ms. Bradley loved me, I began to trust her. I started to open up. I wasn't afraid of getting hurt by her because now I felt comfortable. As the first year went by, I slowly began to accept her.

We would have long conversations together every night. Ms. Bradley said, "You can come and talk to me about anything, anytime. You don't have to worry about holding back your feelings, because I can understand."

We didn't have to have a reason to talk. We'd talk like best friends talk. I told her everything about my life and she would tell me everything about hers. She tried to help me benefit from her experience.

We respected one another because we had similar backgrounds. She had a rough childhood, just like me. Her mother didn't want her, just like mine didn't want me.

The only difference was that Ms. Bradley hadn't been in foster care when she was a child. She lived with other family members. I guess that's one reason why she never pushed me into calling her "mom." She knew what it was like not to have your real mother. She said that whatever I decided to call her would be just fine.

Everything I was going through, Ms. Bradley had already gone through. She always seemed to know the reason why I did certain things.

If I acted out in school, she would say to me, "Omar, I know how you feel. You're upset because you want to be with your parents. That's why you're acting out, because you have no one else to take it out on."

I would look at her and say to myself, "How does she know what I'm going through?" Then I'd go to my room and think about what she said. When I came back, I'd say to her, "You know, you're right."

I used to rebel against everyone who wanted to get close to me. I had been hurt by a lot of people, so I had made up my mind never to get hurt again. Ms. Bradley felt the same exact way when she was my age.

I lived with her for about eight months before I finally called her mom. The first time I called her that, the look on her face was like the moon shining. It wasn't all that hard calling her mom. When that happened, we both knew I had finally accepted her.

Ms. Bradley never pushed me into calling her "mom." She knew what it was like not to have your real mother.

I lived with Ms. Bradley for three years. During those three years I became a happier person as my self-esteem grew. But when I was 16, the time came when I had to choose between going back home to my aunt and uncle or getting adopted by Ms. Bradley.

Ms. Bradley wasn't pressuring me to get adopted and she wasn't insisting that I go. If she adopted me, I would still have full contact and visitation with my aunt and uncle. The choice was mine to make.

I remember one thing Ms. Bradley told me before I made my decision. She said, "Omar, if you leave, I'm still gonna love you like my own, but you know that once you go you can't come back."

It hurt inside to know that if I went home to my family and messed up, I couldn't have a second chance to come back to live with her.

I didn't understand why she said this, but through writing in my journal I answered my question. You can't come into someone's life, have a heavy impact on them, leave, and then come back whenever you decide. I thought what Ms. Bradley said was fair, because I wouldn't want anyone doing that to me.

I finally decided to go back home to my aunt and uncle, even though everyone was telling me it wouldn't work out. Although I loved Ms. Bradley, I was scared to get adopted. I always had my heart set on going back home to my aunt and uncle and this was my final chance to be with them. I wanted to give it a shot. I felt like I had to prove I could make it with my own family. Ms. Bradley was very understanding and respected my decision.

I felt so empty as I was packing up my clothes, because she had helped me buy some of them.

After I left, I used to wonder, "Omar, did you make the right decision by deciding to go back home to your aunt and uncle?"

For a long time I couldn't answer that question, but now, looking back, I know I made a big mistake. When I got home to my aunt and uncle, I realized I had grown into a new person with Ms. Bradley. I had changed, but my aunt and uncle hadn't.

I needed a certain kind of love that my family couldn't give me. I couldn't go to my aunt and uncle with my problems. I couldn't be friends with them, like I could with Ms. Bradley. I wanted to go back to her, but I couldn't tell my family that.

I realized Ms. Bradley was the mother that I had always wanted, the family I never had. I wanted both Ms. Bradley and my family, but sometimes you can't have both things.

There was so much tension with my aunt and uncle that I got kicked out of their house a year after I returned. I ended up being bounced from group home to group home for a whole summer before I finally moved in with other relatives.

I don't blame anyone for what happened because it was my decision to go back home. I should have listened to what everyone was saying, but I was too blind to see what they were talking about.

Ms. Bradley is deceased today and it hurts to know that she is gone physically, that I can never see that smile and or hear that laugh again. I no longer have her to talk to when I need some advice or when I do something wrong.

She's not around to tell me the reasons why I behave the way I do, so I can learn how to change. I don't have her shoulder to cry on anymore and I don't have my best friend.

But she is forever in my heart and soul and in every footstep I take. I feel that we are closer now than we ever were before. Maybe not physically, but spiritually. I can sometimes feel her guiding me through all the rough spots as I come upon them. She was and is a blessing to me.

Without her, I would still be just another lost kid in the system.

Love you, Mom.

Your son,

Omar.

Omar was 18 when he wrote this story.

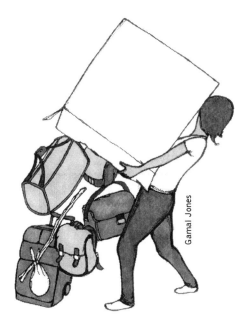

Gamal Jones

Great Expectations

By Hattie Rice

When I move to new placements I usually don't have any expectations, but a year ago I moved to a new foster home and I had a fantasy image in my mind. I pictured my new life as a double chocolate Oreo cookie with a glass of milk. Instead, I ended up with a turkey burger (good and good for ya, but it just ain't the beef).

At the time I was a junior in high school and was living in a group home. When I was told I had to move, I was determined to find a foster mom who could help me get into college, because I knew my books could take me to a better life.

When I met Diane, she seemed like what I was looking for. Diane has a good education—a bachelor's degree and a master's in nursing. She has several jobs: she works as a psychiatric nurse, an editor for a black television station (even though she's white), and has a side hustle in real estate.

Diane is caring, considerate, and sacrificing. She's also systematic, sometimes reminding me of Robocop. She plans everything out (kind of scary) and always thinks that she is right (we all do, but she's extreme).

During the long process of getting to know Diane before I moved in, my hopes rose. She started our first chat by asking about the basics, like my hobbies, relationship with family, interest in going to college, and the career I might enjoy. (Doesn't she sound like a social worker?)

I probed her to find out her reasons for wanting foster kids, and she told me that she could not have kids but wanted to adopt two girls and create a family. She also said she'd had a rocky relationship with her own mother.

Diane and I continued our conversation during a lunch date at an Italian restaurant (I love a good sausage). Soon after, we met with another foster teen, Nef, who was considering moving in, too.

At the restaurant, the three of us talked about what we could expect while living together. When it came to the budget, Diane said, "With the money I receive for y'all, we will figure out a budget. The money you need each month will go in a checking account, and the rest will go in a savings account."

"Whaat! Come one more time again?" I yelled. I must admit that even a cynical character like me was impressed that she was disproving the myth that all foster parents just want the money.

Soon Nef and I stayed at Diane's house for a weekend. I made my cooking debut: turkey burgers, sweet potato fries, and grilled vegetables, which may sound weird but was on point. Afterward Diane showed us how to play Backgammon and Scrabble. I won twice in Backgammon (that was not beginner's luck!) and I lost by one in Scrabble (Diane cheated, I know she did).

In the morning, Diane made breakfast and we headed downtown, where she bought us blue Ralph Lauren sheets and matching Tommy Hilfiger accessories, and we picked out paint and a rug for our new MTV-style crib.

So you can see how, by the time I moved in last summer, I had built a fantasy image in my head of what it was going to be like. I imagined that in our life together I'd be the black Marsha, Nef would be Cindy, the little girl, since she was cute, and Diane would be the Brady Bunch father because he knew the answer to every problem, which was annoying during the show but handy in real life. Somehow I forgot that starting any new family from scratch is going to come with misunderstandings.

> **Somehow I forgot that starting any new family from scratch is going to come with misunderstandings.**

Once Nef and I moved in, things got complicated. Nef dropped out of summer school after getting jaw surgery and they constantly argued about it. Diane wanted her to do something with her summer, or at least get out the house instead of sitting around watching TV. But you know black people—you don't see us till after 6 p.m.

Diane also decided we were moving five blocks because she wanted to buy an apartment. That infuriated me—I'd already moved three times that year. The move was very stressful, and I felt Diane took it out on us, like she also believed we should be Brady Bunch perfect.

When we were painting my new room, I said I wanted to paint some edging burgundy and the rest tan. "Regular people do not do that," Diane replied. You cannot imagine how tight I was. I felt like she was ridiculing me because of my unfortunate beginnings.

I felt the same way when she seemed more interested in showing me her culture—setting the table right and going to ballets—than learning about mine.

Around Diane, I sometimes felt like I was supposed to act like a puppet following her commands. She expected me to do my chores on her schedule, and flipped on me if I was late for school just once. I wanted to tell her, "I had to be a sole survivor just to get by. I don't need you telling me how to do every task."

Even though I had my issues with Diane, I kept quiet while she and Nef argued. Usually I don't get in arguments because I try to stay detached—not let anyone bother me, not face reality, and keep any anger I feel under control.

Laying back was something I learned as a child, because getting upset with my mentally ill parents only hurt their feelings and never resulted in any change. It was easier to detach from the situation than get my hopes up and then get let down.

But as Diane got agitated, it seemed like she was yelling at me for the simplest things. The tension was getting on my nerves, and I also began to take it personally. I think my feelings got hurt and I got angry because I actually cared about making our relationship work. I figured that I had to be willing to get emotionally involved, whether with love or anger.

One day I decided to jump in when she and Nef were already going at it. (I had the best timing, right?) Diane began to get on me about budgets and my complaints about therapy. I screamed, "I went, OK? Who goes to therapy on their birthday?" In my head I was just waiting for her comeback because I was in shutdown mode.

Then she changed the subject, saying that I never told her I was spending the weekend with my best friend. "Either you have a bad memory or I live in an imaginary world," I said.

She picked me shooting a hoop with the Looney Tunes.

I snickered, "Denial is a disease."

She claimed my imagination runs away with me.

I yelled, "Your memory is running away from you and you need to find it." In Elmer Fudd's voice I added, "Which way did it go? Which way did it go?"

By then Diane was furious, too, and basically said that we could get the hell out of her house.

I said, "We have to make a change."

She had the nerve to answer that she's not changing for anyone because this was the way she was when we came and the way she'll be if we decide to leave.

That really hurt me. I often have the feeling that I try so hard to make things work, constantly conforming my beliefs and desires to others, while others don't seem willing to do the same. As a child I didn't go to school because I felt I had to meet the needs of my mentally ill mother. In my group home I never talked about my problems to the social worker, not because I didn't have any but because I felt the other girls needed her more.

Although it was a different situation with Diane, I felt similarly: I'm going to ballets but you can't watch a hip hop video? I'm crying and all you can say is, "I don't care about your feelings right now." I'm tired of having to change myself and take on responsibility that shouldn't fall on me.

I think my feelings got hurt and I got angry because I actually cared about making our relationship work.

Suddenly, I felt toward Diane like I did with my mother: used, pushed to the limit, and unappreciated. I felt like I'd done all I could and she didn't see how hard I tried. Seeing our relationship start to crumble despite my efforts caused me a mean mini life crisis.

After the argument, I laughed, not because I found it humorous but because my intuition told me the situation would go bad and I felt sad but didn't want to show it. My laugh signified nervousness. I was nervous that living with Diane would not work out and I'd have to find a series of places to live, giving less of myself each move.

Our social worker recommended family therapy. To me, it was a waste of time. Nef and Diane argued and seemed to ignore the therapist's advice as if she wasn't conducting the sessions. Even if they spoke calmly, their faces showed the opposite. During the sessions, I was more spaced out than Buzz Lightyear.

But one night we had a heart to heart. I was open with Diane.

I told her how I felt under-appreciated because she criticizes me. (Hello, I've had more than enough of that! And I already have low self-esteem.) I also said I was feeling alienated because some tiny remote part of my heart (when I say tiny, I mean smaller than Michael Jackson's nose) cared for them and didn't want us to be so angry at each other.

After the discussion I felt relieved, not because I believed things were going to get better, but because I was able to express my feelings rather than keep everything bottled up inside.

The next day when I got to therapy everybody I'd ever met at the agency was there. They told me they'd decided Nef should leave the home. I think all three of us were shocked. We went the rest of the week without arguing, just making the best of our last week together. She started packing while Diane and I prepared for our new life, just the two of us.

Nef moved out on a Sunday. When I walked her out, I felt happy to see her go someplace where she might feel more comfortable, and scared because this was the moment of truth for Diane and me. And you know what? Since then we've had no major arguments, just little discussions about the budget sheets and chores. My emotions, which were once like an Oklahoma twister, now feel calm and serene.

Looking back, I think some of my anger toward Diane was just my feelings about my mom spilling out because I've never confronted my family with how they made me feel down and depressed. Instead, I tried to ignore my feelings. But when I confronted Diane, I was probably taking all the anger of my childhood out on her.

I've also realized that it's time for me to let go of my technique of staying detached. For years that technique allowed me to not let anyone's feelings disturb my composure, but it's become a problem for me that I'm constantly hiding behind my shield of security. To get close to Diane, I've had to make the transition to actually caring, and as weird as it may sound, that's a really big step for me.

Even though this adjustment has made me so uncomfort-able, slowly I see that I'm getting more comfortable. Ever since I entered foster care at 14, I've kept a big box full of bags in my room just in case I needed to move out. I never expected to have a home or to feel stable.

But one day Diane politely asked me, "Could you clean out that big box in your room?" Inside I was hollering, "No! No! No!" But surprisingly, I decided to rid myself of all that extra baggage. (It helped that I had Remy Ma's "I'm Conceited" playing in the background to boost me up.) I felt safe and secure throwing those bags away, confident about where I was at in my life, and proud that I'm trying not to let my past experiences control my life.

Hattie was 17 when she wrote this story.
She later attended SUNY Binghamton.

Not What a Foster Parent Should Be

By Anonymous

My first foster mother, Hazel, had a beautiful house, laden with all types of beautiful, expensive items and furniture. The house was always clean, the kitchen floor was always waxed so that it would shine, and the refrigerator was always full.

The bedrooms were also kept neat and clean. My room, which was on the second floor, had no door, but it was satisfactory and the beds were very fancy. The attic was like a big dorm room with five girls, five beds, dressers, and a television in the center of the room.

The basement was an apartment for her daughter and grandchildren. All in all, it was a spectacular house to live in.

In the morning, we all ate together. Same with lunch and dinner. We had it made (or so we thought). At one time our house had 15 people in all: my foster mother and father, her daughter, her four grandchildren, three adopted girls, and five foster children.

All who were capable took turns washing the dishes and we all had our assigned chores. Mine was to do the bathroom and keep my room clean. Things were so good that we even had regular snacks and dessert after meals. I thought, "Wow, what a life!"

So why am I complaining? Why am I not still living there?

Hazel could not relate to some of the things that the foster kids in her house had been through. She didn't understand the abuse we experienced and the effect it had on our personalities. So she often made ignorant comments and criticized our reasons for responding the way we did when certain problems arose in our lives. While we had adequate food and shelter, we didn't have the understanding and patience we needed.

While we had adequate food and shelter, we didn't have the understanding and patience we needed.

When I first moved in, Hazel started to gossip about the other foster girls in the house, even about those who were no longer living there. She often spoke about how mean they were to her, especially the teenagers. Hazel claimed that after the last teenager she had, she did not want any more because we were set in our own ways and difficult to train in the ways she wanted.

When she talked about the other girls in the house, I would only listen and not comment. I never expected my turn to come, when she would talk about me behind my back just like she did the other girls. Hazel always treated me so nicely that I didn't see it coming.

I began to talk to her about my past, the problems I had living with my parents, the abuse I suffered at the hands of my father. Hazel acted as if she understood how I was feeling and how it affected me. Because of the abuse, I became someone who stayed by myself and kept everything that bothered me inside. That's the society I came from.

I n the West Indies it is very uncommon for people to talk about certain personal problems, such as abuse. You see, even if people know that something is wrong, it is very rare for people to become involved. Instead they will "mind their own business." What's worse is if the person who is victimizing someone else holds a respectable position in society. Then it either "never happened" or it is kept quiet.

Hazel and I were from different cultures, so she did not understand what life had been like for me in the West Indies. I trusted Hazel like she was my own grandmother, but she disappointed me with her attitude.

One day I overheard her telling one of her friends about my abusive past and how I was struggling to deal with it.

"Girl," Hazel said to her friend, "she's from another country and she's here 'cause her father molested her, and she didn't say anything about it till she was older. She's just always so sad and depressed that sometimes it irks me. I can't understand how her mother did not do anything about it. And her mother still lives with him, you know! Girl, I tell you, I would have picked up my bags and be gone."

I could not believe that she could be so cruel and insensitive. How could she talk about me like that? I began to have hateful feelings toward her, but I didn't show them. I didn't want my caseworker or anyone at the agency to think that I loved to complain about her. After all, she claimed that she had a very good reputation within our agency.

Hazel also talked about a 15-year-old girl who lived in the house. Hazel told me that Sonia was slow in learning and would never be able to do anything for herself because she couldn't read or write well. I decided to make an effort to help Sonia read and write so that she could pass her classes.

One time Hazel said to Sonia, "You could do it if you really wanted to." Then she said to me, "She can't never learn properly. She's too slow. I don't know how she got so far into high school not knowing how to read and write. She must not have wanted to learn."

I never believed that because when I began to teach Sonia, she was so eager to learn (although very frustrated because it was difficult for her to learn at age 15). But instead of encouraging Sonia, I would hear Hazel telling the other kids, "Better learn your work. Otherwise you will end up like Sonia and never be able to do anything for yourself."

When Sonia was not around, Hazel would call her lazy and slow, but when she was in the room Hazel would tell her how good she was. Many times I would hear her talk about Sonia and felt sorry for her.

One day I overheard my foster mother telling one of her friends about my abusive past.

She also talked about Kayla, another girl who once lived there and was my roommate. Kayla was 13 and had a baby who lived in another foster home. The other girls in the house didn't know this, but I did because Hazel told me.

The fact that Kayla had a baby was supposed to be confidential, yet when Kayla was not around my foster mother would make comments like: "How could she be having sex at such a young age to end up with a baby? So she likes boys, huh? She's so big for her age and eats so much, soon she has to go 'cause I won't be able to feed her. I tell you, girls these days are so full of heat."

Hazel was the opposite of what a foster parent should be. It's bad enough that she gossiped about us, but what's worse is what she said. As a foster parent, and even more so as a parent who had kids of her own, she should never have made those negative comments.

When someone decides to become a foster parent, she should realize that she's going to be taking in youth who have had difficult experiences and she should be prepared to deal with these children. Foster parents should be selected and trained to deal with abused and neglected children.

After spending a little more than a year in Hazel's "mansion," I left and moved to another home where my new foster parents are truly parents.

Hazel had some good qualities. She made sure that we were always clean and well-kept. She always made sure that we were fed and that the house was clean and tidy. But she didn't know what was most important about being a foster parent.

She would often say to us that we would never find a home as good as hers once we left.

Well, guess what? I found a loving and supportive foster home, so I guess I proved her wrong.

The writer was 19 when she wrote this story.
She attended John Jay College.

Gary Smith

She's Gay—and the Best Foster Mom I Know

By Arelis Rosario

My sister has the sweetest foster mother alive. Her name is Mary, and when I go to her house every Sunday to visit I feel overcome with happiness.

I always play football, basketball, and kickball in Mary's backyard with my brothers and sisters. Her house is the best of all the foster homes I've seen because Mary treats her foster children like they're her own. In other foster homes, they treat you like you're a foreigner. In some homes you have to share your room with like four other kids, but in Mary's house everyone has her own room. Some foster parents punish you by hitting, but Mary uses mediation to resolve problems.

Whenever I see Mary, she always seems happy. She's usually busy because she works out of her home, but when she sees me she always smiles and gives me lots of kisses and hugs. She'll talk to me about regular things, like how my day is going. I'll say, "Pretty OK. Thanks for asking." It's just little stuff, but it's nice to know that she cares.

Part of the reason I like going to Mary's so much is the house itself. As soon as you step inside you're speechless, because it's just so mellow. Mary's house has three floors, five bathrooms, a living room on each floor, a library, and a back and front yard. Mary has five foster children living in her house, but there's a lot of space and it's really peaceful. One of my favorite places is the porch because Mary has a rocking chair there, and when I sit on it I feel like the world freezes and I feel free. Even though I've been to her house many times, every time I go I like to wander around. When I do, my mind finds peace and I can think.

Mary's house is proof that there are foster parents with kind hearts and lots of love to give.

Since I am in foster care and have no one to spend the holidays with, Mary always invites me. Last year I spent Christmas at her house. When I arrived, she told me that they decided to buy a small tree and told me to go see if I could find it. When I stepped into the hallway, my heart stopped as I looked at a beautiful tree covered with angels and red and blue ornaments and icicles. The tree must have stood at least nine feet high. It was the most beautiful tree I had ever seen, and on top was a star that glowed so brightly that I had to shade my eyes.

Mary was standing there smiling at me. I was truly speechless. Next I looked under the tree. It had lots and lots of presents. Many of them were for me. I told my sister that this was the best Christmas I had ever had and she agreed.

There are lots of things I love about Mary—her thoughtfulness, her cheerfulness, even the way she dresses. Mary is also a lesbian, which is fine with me.

When I first met Mary I figured she was gay because she

wore a rainbow necklace and she had gay flags in her house. Many people look down on people who are gay or lesbian, but Mary has made a huge difference in my life. I will always love her for it and will always be grateful.

For the most part, Mary is highly regarded in my foster care agency, but there are a few social workers who don't really like the idea of gay and lesbian foster parents in the system. They don't say it, but you can tell by the unfriendly way they treat Mary.

I think they should be more worried about foster parents who have no love to give. I was in three different foster homes growing up, and two out of the three were really crappy. The foster parents had no respect for the children they were taking care of. In those homes, no one had any love to give a child. For most of my life, what I saw in the world made me feel pretty hopeless. Mary's house is proof that there are foster parents with kind hearts and lots of love to give.

I think part of the problem today is that people think that kids need to be raised 'by their own kind.'

A few months ago I went with Mary to a meeting sponsored by a gay parents' group to encourage gay and lesbian people to become foster parents and to encourage agencies to recruit gay foster parents. The Administration for Children's Services say its policy is not to discriminate based on sexual orientation and they do go out of their way to recruit gay parents, hosting meetings and passing out information at gay events. I am glad to know that the system is doing what it can to make sure there are more foster parents to choose from.

Can a gay man or woman raise a straight child? Can a white man or woman raise a black child? I think so. I think part of the problem today is that people think that kids need to be raised "by their own kind."

Well, Mary isn't only a lesbian. She's also Irish, but she has a house full of kids of different races. She has Korean, Puerto Rican, African-American, and white children, and she loves them all. She's a white, gay woman, and she's the best foster mother I've ever seen.

Arelis was 15 when she wrote this story.
She attended Boston University.

Frank Malkum

Rewriting the Script

By Alex Withers

Here I am in this Salvation Army van on my way to my first foster home with nothing to call my own. It's 1 o'clock in the morning and I feel restless and annoyed, with a twist of anxiety. We turn onto a beautiful, quiet block in Bushwick, a neighborhood in Brooklyn, New York. I get out of the car and my caseworker leads the way.

A chubby lady with an overlapping belly opens the front door and I step in cautiously. She has messy hair and her teeth are yellowed. She kinda looks like the Grinch who stole Christmas. Like it or not, this is my new foster mother.

When the Administration for Children's Services (ACS) picked me up from school earlier that day, I felt like my freedom was snatched while I wasn't looking. They told me that my mother had been arrested, so my younger brother Alan, little sister Cearra, and I had to go to a foster home.

I didn't know what to expect. All I had heard about the system was that children often fought, stole, and got into trouble with each other. I couldn't believe this was happening to me. Would I ever see my mother again?

I felt like the system had just interrupted an interesting story I was telling to a friend—my story. Now I had to start following their story line. It would take a while before I figured out how to write my own script.

After we'd lived with our foster mother Rose (not her real name) for about a month, my siblings opened up to her, but I was still careful. I wasn't shy, but I didn't completely trust her.

Slowly, though, even I felt relaxed enough to start speaking more openly. She told us to call her Aunt Rose, and she always asked about my day in school. We talked about all of the normal things like we were family, and even joked around. It was at times like those that I liked her, but I was still unsure. Something about her bothered me.

When I decided to sell one of my portable video games to buy a pair of sneakers, I found out my instincts about Rose had been right.

Money was scarce for me and I always found myself free-loading, or feeling uncomfortable in my dingy, baggy hand-me-downs from Rose's older nephew. So I sold the game and got $40. The next day after school I went to a store with my friends to pick out a nice pair of Converse.

I was walking home, feeling proud. When I reached the block, though, I saw Rose hanging out of the window with her lips curled up and her eyebrows frowning angrily.

"Where have you been?" she demanded. Without waiting for me to explain, she said, "You know what, I'm getting you outta my house—I ain't got time for this bull—he comin' in here thinkin' he grown."

After that, I started to feel betrayed, and I kept completely to myself. The fact was I hadn't done anything wrong, but she made me feel as though I had.

I guess I could have told the agency, but it was my first foster home and I didn't know my rights. I didn't know if my complaint would be taken seriously. So instead, I just closed myself up like an envelope. I wished I could mail myself back to my mom.

After that episode, things changed. Rose became stern and started setting traps for us. Sometimes, she kept Alan, Cearra, and me in one particular part of the house like it was a children's jail, as if she didn't want to know we lived in her house.

It was my first foster home and I didn't know my rights. I didn't know if my complaint would be taken seriously.

Other times, she seemed suspicious and wanted to control our every move. Like the time when she told Alan and me not to go through the door connecting our room with the living room. We agreed not to use it, even though it was the easiest way for us to exit the house.

One day, Rose called me to bring her a basket of decorations, but I had to go through the forbidden door to get it. Just before I reached the door, I looked down and froze. There in the doorway were a bunch of thumbtacks neatly faced up, about to prick my foot. For a second, I wondered if I was hallucinating. Then I realized that Rose had put them there as a trap for my brother and me, thinking we were going to sneak through the door.

I stared at the thumbtacks. Then I stepped over them and got the basket. I brought it to Rose without saying a word.

When I told my brother what had happened, we weren't sure what to do. We decided to pretend we hadn't seen Rose's little trap. We didn't want to give her the satisfaction. But one of her friend's foster daughters came across the street to hang out and noticed it, too, and brought it up with Rose. Rose was afraid the girl would go to her foster mom and word would get back to the agency.

Rose looked worried and said, "If the worker comes, just say that the thumbtacks spilled on the floor, OK?" So we agreed to that, hoping she'd just go back in her cave and hibernate. The less we saw of her, the easier our lives were.

After that, Rose began giving Alan and me money, treating us more nicely and staying off our backs so that she'd be covered if the social worker came and started asking questions.

The worker never did ask about the thumbtacks, and I didn't know how to bring it up. Rose always screened our phone conversations, so I had no privacy with my social worker when she called. And I didn't think trying to talk one on one with Rose would have made a difference.

So we played the game right along with Rose, even though deep inside we wanted to tell. I knew the situation was never going to get better by playing along. But I didn't have any other ideas.

Going to school and seeing my friends helped me to forget about all this. My friends were like a family, and we had overwhelming times together just laughing away the painful experiences. That's how Alan and I endured, until things suddenly escalated.

One night during a barbecue at the house, Alan went to the store and didn't come back. When Rose found out, she started playing that same old record, talking about Alan and me as if we were sub-human.

"They fight each other, they bite each other," she started.

Some girl said, "Don't talk about him as if he ain't right there...are you OK, boy?"

I nodded. It took everything I had to keep from going on a rampage. Seriously, because Rose was talking about us like we were animals.

Rose finished with her favorite line: "I ain't puttin' up with this. I'm taking them back to the agency tomorrow!"

I thought she was just being loud to show off, but I hoped she really meant it this time, because I was ready to leave. We were just raggedy foster children to her. Being a foster parent was just profit for Rose.

The next morning she drove us to the agency, silent all the way. When we started the meeting, the caseworker and supervisor actually tried to throw my brother and me back with her. After everything, they were like, "Let's give it another chance," like, Boys, you're gonna behave this time, right? The blame was always on us.

I wanted to gather up my family, jump Rose, and trash the agency, but I told myself it wasn't that serious. I didn't even tell the staff all the things that Rose had done to us. Since I had played along with it, I figured they would think I was lying.

Finally, they made their decision. My brother and I were going to a new home and Rose would keep Cearra. I was irate. Not only did the agency take her side over ours without asking any questions, they had decided to leave my sister (who was 7 at the time) all alone with that confusing lady. How would Rose treat Cearra without my brother and me around to protect her?

At the agency, the blame was always on us.

I wasn't going to just sit there like a lump on a log and watch my family fall apart after all of the bull I'd been put through. I brainstormed about the best ways to outdo Rose without getting into trouble myself. I felt like talking wouldn't get me very far, so I decided I had to plan something strong.

It took me a while to come up with just the right idea. And then…Yes! I had it. I decided to write a formal letter about my experience at Rose's house and how she'd insulted my dignity and integrity. I'd tell it all, from the moment we introduced ourselves to the last time she cursed us out. It was a nice, lengthy letter, and I felt proud to show it. I gave everyone I knew a copy, including my new caseworker and the new supervisor.

They were so surprised and commended me for my maturity

and good writing. As a result of the letter, Cearra was taken out of Rose's home. What's more, my caseworker told me that from now on, no child protective agency in the U.S. would allow Rose to so much as babysit if a background check was involved.

I felt relieved, like I'd regained a little bit of control in my life. Even though we're still not all together under the same roof, I was proud that I'd stood up for myself and protected my family. I went to bed that night with a smile on my face.

I've moved on from Rose's house into a much better foster home, but this ordeal taught me some things that I won't forget. When I first went into care, I felt powerless, and my only weapon was avoidance. Instead of trying to change the situation, I kept to myself. This experience showed me that you can resolve issues without resorting to negative tactics. Now I'm starting to see that there are things I can do to take charge and make positive changes in my life.

Alex was 15 when he wrote this story. He later joined the Youth Justice Board, a teen advocacy group that works to improve policies affecting young people in New York City.

She's Not in It for the Money

By Jeffrey Allan Culbertson

One summer in June, my sister and I moved out of kinship care and into a foster home with a woman named Pauline. When I first met Pauline at the agency, my little sister Jennifer had already been living with her for a couple of days. Pauline arrived at the agency wearing a navy blue business suit with her hair done up impressively. After introductions, we went to her house. I had everything I owned with me.

I was nervous. I had so many things going through my head, questions like: Where was Pauline from? What would she be like as a foster parent? Was she clean? Could she cook? Where would I sleep? Did I have to do chores? If so, would I get paid for performing them? (Just kidding.)

I was anxious partly because of what I had seen on TV about foster care, like instances of foster parents beating, neglecting, and starving their foster kids. Pauline didn't seem to be that type of person, but I knew that looks could be deceiving.

Pauline took me on a tour of the house. She showed me the bathroom, her room, Jennifer's new room, and the kitchen. I noticed the pink carpet that covered the entire first floor. Now I am not a big fan of pink, but I thought it looked nice in the house. The antique artwork and furniture in the living room made the house seem classy.

Then Pauline showed me downstairs to the basement where I would live. It was a very spacious one-bedroom apartment with a nice-sized kitchen, a nice bathroom, and a huge living room. There were beautiful paintings of scenery on the walls and the furniture was tasteful. I knew I would easily adjust to all the space, even though it would be a change from my old home.

I was anxious because of what I had seen on TV about foster parents neglecting their foster kids.

The day after I moved in with Pauline was my junior high school graduation. After graduation, Pauline was waiting at home for me with open arms and a graduation gift. We talked about my school year. Her kindness was confusing—I had thought that all foster parents were only in it for the money. I was beginning to think I was wrong.

The next night, Pauline, Jennifer, and I all sat down to the dinner table and ate a wonderful meal that Pauline had cooked. As we ate, we talked about living together. I asked questions about curfew, chores, and what my boundaries were in the house. I was still surprised that I had the entire basement to myself. It gave me a feeling of freedom.

When Pauline said I had no curfew, I felt my boundaries expand even more. Pauline also said she was very strict on schoolwork, and the importance of conducting ourselves respectfully in the house and anywhere else. I thought that there were not too many rules, so I respected Pauline by doing as she said. Since then, we've had few problems.

Slowly, we got to know each other. Shopping, eating, and watching TV together gave us a sense of each other and what we were all about. Since Pauline is a real estate agent, my interest in opening my own real estate agency also helped us get close. She is showing me how to go about reaching my goal.

Over the nearly two years I've been with Pauline, I've learned that she's a forgiving and compassionate person, and tries to make people happy by showing her love in many ways. In turn, Pauline has learned that I am a kind, generous person, but I can't tolerate too many people (which is why I dislike group homes). And Pauline has taught me how to have more tolerance by being patient with people who I don't like.

Her kindness was confusing— I thought that all foster parents were only in it for the money.

Now, Pauline is more than a foster mother—she is a real mother to me. She showed me love no one else had given to me. She gave me the assurance that I could do positive things with my life, even without my biological parents. Because of this, living with Pauline has been the best thing that has ever happened to me. And I now realize that what the TV and newspapers say about foster care is often just the bad side.

Sooner or later I will have to decide whether to go with my parents or stay with Pauline. I haven't decided, but I am leaning toward staying with Pauline. No matter what, I will always love my parents. But since things have gotten tense between us, I'd rather stay with Pauline.

Jeffrey was 16 when he wrote this story.

Getting Hurt All Over Again

By Arelis Rosario

I was 4 when my siblings and I entered our first foster home. In that home, our foster mother would lock us in a room for hours at a time. She called it "the playroom," but in fact it was just an empty room with nothing in it. She also said she believed in good nutrition. What that meant was that if we didn't eat, she would force feed us.

The worst thing I remember was what she did to my younger sister. My sister was only 2 years old when we went into care and doesn't remember, but I remember the times that lady would push her down the stairs. Maybe she was angry, or maybe she was crazy, or maybe she just thought it was funny. I really don't know. I was in that home until I was 7 years old, and during all that time the abuse continued.

When we had our monthly visits, we would complain to

our mother about the home, and she complained to our social worker, but our social worker told her that there were no homes willing to take four siblings, so we either had to stay in that home or get split up.

We finally left because the courts said my mother was ready to have us back. I was happy, but my mother really wasn't ready to have us back. Life with my mother was bad and, at age 14, I went back into care.

The day that I went to my second foster home, the smell of urine filled the elevator. A little old lady was my new foster mother. She was Puerto Rican and she only spoke Spanish. I am also Puerto Rican and I speak a little Spanish, but I didn't tell them that because I like to hear what people say when they think you can't understand. Instead, we communicated through her daughter Mona.

Living in that home, I felt crowded all the time. I had to share a room with my foster mother and my two other foster sisters, and my foster mother's niece when she stayed over. Sometimes they would take my covers and I would have to sleep in the cold night air. In total there were six people who lived there officially and four other people who constantly spent the night. So there were really 10 of us, and only three bedrooms in this crowded apartment in the projects.

My social worker came to check on me the first week I was there, and my foster mother asked me to lie and say that only four people lived there. After that, I really began to question whether this was going to be a decent place for me to live.

Soon after that, they began to talk about me in Spanish. The things they said really hurt. They would call me "una perra" (a dog) and they would say I was ugly and fat. Then my foster mother's niece began to steal my stuff, and I did not have a lot of stuff to begin with. Her niece and nephew would also hit me and pull my hair, and my foster brother often yelled at me. One time I asked my social worker if I would get clothing money, and she said she'd just sent the check to my foster mother. When I got home and asked about the money, Mona said she bought me clothes and that they would have to last, but the clothes she gave me looked like hand-me-downs. I was furious.

After about a week, my foster mother never let me outside the house except to go to school. My curfew was 4 o'clock in the afternoon, which gave me time to walk home from school and that's it. She said that teenagers were a hassle and she didn't want me to get used to having too much freedom and staying out until all hours of the night. Sometimes my teacher would hold me back for tutoring and my foster mother would call the police and my social worker so that I could be found. When I was in her home, I would sit and look out the window. I felt like I was in jail.

Eventually, I decided I was going to escape. When it was

Mona said she bought me clothes, but they looked like hand-me-downs. I was furious.

time for me to go to school, I went to my agency instead. I told my social worker all about my curfew, my foster brother yelling at me, the stealing, and about the time they told me to lie. She was shocked and called my foster home to ask if all this was true. Of course my foster mother said no and began to lie about me. She said I stole her son's beeper and that I was the one lying. When I heard this I yelled, "Even if you pay me, I swear I will never go back to that home."

My social worker questioned me to see if I was lying and also checked my bag to see if I had stolen anything, which made me mad. Eventually, though, she told me that I only had to stay there two more weeks. I said fine, but I couldn't stand it. So later that week, I spent the night at my friend's house and returned to my foster home the next day at 2 a.m. My foster mom was mad at me for what I'd done. I said, "I don't give a damn." Then she called my social worker, said she wanted me out, and I was moved the next day. Boy, was I glad to leave that place.

I know not all foster homes are as bad as the first two I was in, because the third foster home I was placed in was better. The girls in that home had some issues they needed to solve. They would lie, fight, and steal, so it wasn't so fun to be there. But at least the foster parents in my new home cared about me and how I was doing. My foster mother always asked how I was and always came to my school to pick me up when I was sick. She gave me my clothing money in my hand. She was a good foster mother to me. My sister's foster mother is the greatest foster mother you could wish for, which is more evidence for me that not all foster parents are bad, not all foster homes are crappy. But from what I've seen, there are too many bad homes and not enough good homes.

From what I've seen, there are too many bad foster homes and not enough good ones.

If you doubt me, my evidence goes on and on. One of my friends told me that her foster mother used to hit her with switches of sugar cane and that her foster father treated her like she was a slave, making her cook and clean because his wife was too old to do it. Another of my friends told me that when her foster mother got mad at her, she would hit her face against the wall until she started to bleed. Luckily, after my friends had lived in their foster homes for a while, both homes were closed. But some bad homes stay open.

For instance, the first foster home I was in remained open. I know because once when I was in my agency, I overheard another girl complaining about the same home to my social worker. And when my brother and sister reported problems with one home they were in, they were moved but the home stayed open.

In that home, their foster mother was stealing their clothes, my sister's rings, and gifts they received for Christmas. Her children would hit my siblings and pull my sister's hair. My brother, who was raised always to watch out for his siblings, would get into fights with her sons and they would jump him. When my brother complained to his foster mother, she did nothing about it.

My brother and sister told my mother and their social worker. My brother was removed first, then my sister. They were removed because of the problems they reported, but also because they were failing most of their classes and because their foster mother wouldn't bring them to the agency for their mandatory visits. But when my sister went back for the rest of her clothes, there were already other foster children who had taken their places.

Why is the system taking kids and putting them in even worse homes than the ones they came from? If I reported problems in a foster home and they removed me because of those problems, then how can they turn around and sweep my report under the rug when it comes to the next group of kids?

I know there aren't enough good foster homes to take in all the kids in the system. But this really can't be an excuse for putting kids into homes where they're going to be mistreated. It would be better if the agencies admitted they had a problem and closed all the bad homes. Then maybe the system would start getting serious about figuring out creative ways of finding decent foster homes, rather than putting us in the care of "parents" who are going to hurt us all over again.

Arelis was 17 when she wrote this story.
She attended Boston University.

YC Art Dept.

The Other Side of the Story

By Natasha Santos

A few months ago, I visited Circle of Support, a monthly meeting for foster parents in New York City. I expected to find a few old ladies shaking their heads and grumbling about how hard it is to be a foster parent, saying things like, "Why did I do this?" and "Kids these days have no respect!" and "I can't wait to retire." What I discovered instead was a group of women who come together to get advice and give support to other members of Club Foster Parent.

I was curious to hear what foster parents have to say about the kids they take care of, and I wanted to know how Circle of Support helps them. As I spoke to the foster parents, many things they said reminded me of what foster children say, like that the system makes them feel isolated, helpless, or abandoned at times, or that they feel shifted around and ask for support they don't get.

Despite that, they also described forming intensely close bonds with the kids in their care. Fostering has had an unexpectedly difficult but rewarding impact on their lives. The half dozen women gathered around the table seemed both comfortable and anxious about discussing the night's topic—talking to your teenagers about sex.

One of the first foster parents to arrive was Lourdes Alvarez, who is middle-aged but looks about 20 years younger. Lourdes has a blunt tongue but an easy manner. She has been a foster parent for about 17 years, taking after her mother, who was a foster parent while Lourdes was growing up.

Lourdes began to foster once her own boys grew up and didn't want to hang out with her anymore. She said that she felt lonely, so she decided to get foster kids. She chose to take in kids with serious medical or mental illnesses because she thought she had the patience to handle their needs.

The presenter that night was Shawnese Parker, who has four teen girls at home, one biological and three adopted. Shawnese was in foster care herself, so when she became a foster parent she felt that she had something unique to offer the kids she took in. "I learned from my experiences," Shawnese told me.

Shawnese said she became a foster parent partly because she wanted more kids, but it seemed complicated to give birth again since she's gay. "As my daughter got a little bit older, I felt that it was wrong for her not to have someone to play with," she said. "But asking a dude to have a baby with me wasn't OK with me."

While Shawnese prefers having teens in her home, Lourdes said that teens worry her. Lourdes takes children between 3 and 10. "Younger kids are more controllable, you can guide them more," she told me. "Some teens have been through so much. They don't trust, they don't believe in themselves. It's like pulling teeth."

Lourdes and Shawnese both have had many kids in their

houses—"over 60," Shawnese told me. The most rewarding relationships were with children who stayed long enough to grow, they said.

"Some kids come so sad, so fragile. They can't read, they're not at their age level, they're not climbing or jumping, they're withdrawn," Lourdes said. "You give them the proper attention, love, physical and play therapy. You see them go from withdrawn to speaking up. You see a child getting better."

One of Shawnese's most rewarding but difficult relationships is with an adopted daughter who has a mental illness. Shawnese didn't know how to handle her behavior and found it hard to find help from the system when she needed it.

In 17 years of fostering, Lourdes has only asked the agency to remove one child from her home.

One time, when her adopted children were young, that daughter and another child duct-taped the baby-sitter's arms and legs together while she slept on the floor, then wilded out around the house.

Then the daughter killed the family bird and dog, and set fire to the toy box. "When I asked her why she did it, she said because she heard the devil tapping outside her window. It was a tree branch," Shawnese said. "I knew I needed help. That's just not normal."

Shawnese felt her adoptive daughter's home visits should stop for a while. "A lot of it had to do with seeing her parents," she said. "She went to spend time with them, and when she came back home, I could see the difference." But the agency didn't agree. "They didn't want to listen to me even though I'd spent three years with this child."

Shawnese got so frustrated that she asked the agency to temporarily place the girl in a residential treatment center, but the agency threatened to take all of her kids out of her home. Then she tried to get her daughter evaluated by a psychiatrist and into therapy, but the foster care agency wasn't helpful.

Finally she called the Administration for Children's Services, which supervises the foster care agencies, and said that she was a lawyer "representing Shawnese Parker." The next day, her foster care agency finally responded and she got the help she needed. For a while all of them went to family therapy, and her daughter is still in therapy to this day.

Lourdes also has been through a lot with some of the kids in her care, especially since she takes kids with the greatest needs. One girl who came to Lourdes at 4 years old was disabled and mentally retarded. Now, at 21, she still wears diapers and is on a feeding tube. Another child has a life-threatening illness and was put in care because he wasn't getting the medicine he needed at home. Others simply have difficult behaviors or are recovering from severe abuse.

In 17 years of fostering, Lourdes has only asked the agency to remove one child from her home. "I had a 3-year-old who destroyed my house. He was very, very hyper, and he was emotionally disturbed. I couldn't control him, and even the little ones can do damage," she said. "He'd tear his own clothes, scratch himself up, pull the other kids' hair, bang his head on the floor, and scream and scream. He broke the TV and VCR. He broke a bed, put holes in the walls, and would beat up the other kids—even a 10-year-old!"

Lourdes asked that he be put on medication to calm him down so he could control himself, but the agency said he was too young. "After five months I couldn't deal," Lourdes told me. "All the other kids were suffering. It was not fair to them. He needed to be in a home where it was only him, with a foster parent who could devote all the attention to him."

Even years later, Lourdes sounded sad when she remembered that little boy. "He was beautiful. I felt so bad for him," she told me. "There was nothing else I could do. I'd had a couple of the other kids for a long time."

Shawnese and Lourdes said one of the hardest parts of being a foster parent is having to break a relationship with a child you've had living in your home for years. "Some kids you never see again. It hurts. Sometimes you just want to know how they're doing," Lourdes told me.

After kids return to their biological parents, foster parents have no right to see them again. "I had one sibling group for a year before they went back home," Lourdes said. "One day I was shopping and I saw them with their mom. I said, 'Hi' but the parent didn't want them talking to me. She was like, 'Just say hello and keep moving!' These kids were in my house for a year!" The shock and hurt were evident in her voice.

Lourdes said that it's easiest for everyone if the foster parent and the biological family can find some common ground while the child is in care, and keep in touch once the child returns home. Some biological parents have come to her house for dinner or for visits with their kids.

It's not easy to be in care, and it's not easy to be a foster parent either.

"If you have bio parents that can work with you, it helps. I worked with one biological mother—if her kid was bad during the week, she would scold him, 'You gotta listen to Lourdes,'" she said. She still regularly sees some kids once they go home.

The great thing that these two foster parents and many foster kids have in common is that, although they've had difficult experiences, they are still determined and giving. Talking to these parents and looking back on my own life, I had to marvel at our perseverance. Foster parents and foster kids all need perseverance to withstand the rejection we often face, and to keep trying to connect.

Shawnese is still with her adopted children today because they believed in each other. "We were all determined. We knew that we wanted to stay together," Shawnese said, with a definite lift in her voice.

A lot of people could have given up and decided that the task of parenting a mentally ill child was too much for them, but Shawnese stuck with her and found the help they both needed. Today, her adoptive daughter is doing much better—she's a student with a 90 average.

Both of these women have used their own experiences to help others. Shawnese co-founded a Circle of Support group just for foster parents of LGBTQ youth. Lourdes is an "anchor parent" of Circle of Support and chair of the State Foster Parent Association.

Lourdes said she enjoys coming to Circle of Support because she likes helping people who come to the group with problems. "I enjoy the socializing," she added, smiling, "and I get information that I need sometimes."

Shawnese told me she enjoys giving back to other foster parents who don't know they have rights to get services for their foster kids. "It feels good to be able to guide others," she said. "I felt so alone when I was going through the worst time of my life with the kids, and I didn't know where I could get help," she told me. "It's a great feeling when I hear, 'You know, that number you gave me helped a lot.'"

The day I visited, Shawnese was giving a presentation on how foster parents can teach their teens about sexuality. Not too many foster parents (or parents!) feel good about speaking to their kids about sex, but there was no denying that Shawnese put everyone there at ease. She went about the subject brazenly and with little inhibition, presenting purple dental dams, female and male condoms, and information so detailed that even audacious me cringed in embarrassment.

But the parents were remarkably open, and I soon found myself caught up in their questions and conversation. I couldn't help but smile. By going to the group and getting to know Lourdes and Shawnese, I had discovered a bit more humanity in the system.

Usually teens in care see foster parents as being on the opposite end of the system's spectrum. But in another way I could see us as allies against the harsh, cruel world of foster care. It's not easy to be in care, and it's not easy to be a foster parent either. Maybe if we began to view ourselves more as allies fighting against the hurt and injustice we've been through, we could begin to see our similarities and strengths.

Natasha was 18 when she wrote this story.
She attended the University of New Orleans.

Rafael Manashirov

A Foster Mother From Hell

By Angi Baptiste

I'm 16 and I've been living in a foster home for about a year now. Before that I lived in a group home.

Living in a foster home has been better for me than the group home, because some of the things I had to do in the group home I don't have to do now. For example, I can go to sleep anytime I want. There's no set time to turn on or turn off the TV. And chores don't have to be done every day.

But there are certain things about my foster home that make me feel very unhappy. I have a roof over my head and a hot meal, but no love or affection.

The thing I hate the most is the way my foster parent treats me differently from her biological daughter. She doesn't let me stay on the phone to talk to my friends. She gets mad and says I can stay on the phone for only ten minutes. She unplugs the phone or says that she's gonna use the phone when she's not. But my foster mother lets her biological daughter stay on the phone for an hour at a time.

Sometimes when I'm on the phone, my foster mother tries to listen to my conversation. She stands right in front of me pretending she's looking for something. When she does that I just go to my room, but she still tries to listen to my conversation by standing outside my door. She doesn't do that to her daughter.

Sometimes when my friends call me, my foster mother lies to them and tells them that I'm not home or that I'm sleeping. Sometimes she tells them that they have the wrong number. She even does it right in front of my face.

My foster mother wants to be the only one to use the phone. She says it's her phone and she pays the bills.

Another reason why I hate my foster mother is because she always complains that I don't do anything in the house. She tells me that I'm lazy, even though I usually clean the house every week and weekend. (My foster mother always has little children coming over to the house because she works for a daycare center. They always mess up the place.)

Anyway, my foster mother's biological daughter doesn't do anything to help clean the house. Maybe once in a blue moon.

The very worst thing about my foster mother is that I can't eat without asking her permission. For example, in the morning I have to ask if it's okay to make myself breakfast. For lunch it's the same thing—even to drink I have to ask if it's OK. This makes me feel like I'm homeless, asking for food and money. It makes me feel helpless and disturbed.

She is always putting me on hold when I ask for something to eat. She tells me to wait when I'm starving to death. When I'm fixing myself something to eat, she looks at me like I'm gonna steal the food and go in my room to eat it. And at dinner, she gives me my own plate, cup, and fork that she keeps separate from everyone else's. It's embarrassing.

I get followed everywhere around the house except when I go in my room, but sometimes my foster mother just opens my bedroom door to check on what I'm doing.

I think the reason my foster mother does these things is because I'm not her biological daughter. She always tells me that I'm a stranger living in her house, but that she doesn't want to lose the money she's making off me. She treats me like a nobody, even though I already feel like that. I don't like it when she keeps telling me that, 'cause it makes me feel worse about myself.

The way my foster mother treats me is never gonna change. I tried many times to make the situation better by coming home on time (my curfew is 6 p.m.) or by doing something around the house so she won't be mad at me or hate me. But she still screams at me almost every weekend about something stupid.

The system should make sure that foster mothers are well-trained before they let a child into their home.

For a long time the only thing on my mind was running away. But if I ran away, things would get worse for me and I don't want that. I don't want to start all over again. I've had enough of being in group homes.

I've put up with this treatment for a year, but now I am trying to get moved to a new foster home. What I did was call my caseworker and social worker and tell them about my situation. And I kept on calling them almost every month, until they promised to try to move me to a better placement. I'm still waiting, because it's hard to find foster families that want to take teenagers.

I think the system should make sure that foster mothers are well-trained before they let a child into their home. They should make sure the foster mother is taking the child not only for the money, but because there's a place in her heart to show that she cares. The foster mother should want the foster child to have something good in life and to be happy.

The best advice I can give you kids out there is to never give up. If you have a problem with your group home or foster home and you want to be changed, call your social worker and caseworker and keep bothering them until they move you. If you believe in yourself, then you can stand up for your dignity and your rights.

After my story was published, my editor received a phone call from a social worker who read it and who wanted to help me with my problem. She wanted to put me in a new foster home in her agency.

Not long after that I met the social worker, Ms. Hillary Jones. She told me that she had found a perfect foster home for me, and that the family never had a girl before and had wanted a girl for a long time. We talked about these kinds of things for a while.

A month later I met my new foster family by going on a day visit. At first I was very nervous meeting them, because I was thinking that they probably wouldn't like me and my heart was beating real fast. But I was wrong again.

My new foster family is completely different from my old one. I don't have to ask permission to eat.

They welcomed me in their home with open arms. They treated me like I was already part of the family and I felt the same way.

My new foster family is completely different from my old one. I don't have to ask permission to eat. No one follows me around the house or listens to my phone conversations. I feel very comfortable talking to them. We tell jokes and we laugh.

My new foster parents' names are Mr. and Mrs. Cooper. They are very loving and caring. Most of all, they are funny. They also like to go out places and have a good time, and I like that also. For example, Mr. Cooper likes to go fishing sometimes and that's been a new experience for me.

Mrs. Cooper is a great gospel singer. Every time when we go to church on Sunday and she sings, the people at the church love to hear her voice and ask for more. I wish I could sing just like her.

I used to go to church too, but that was when I was little. I never went with my old foster family because I never felt comfortable going anywhere with them, since we never talked that much and had fun. But I like going to church with my new foster family.

In my old foster home I usually stayed out in front of my building instead of going upstairs to my house, because that's how bored I used to be. When it was time to go home, I would usually be like, "Damn, it's time to get my butt upstairs." And my friends would laugh at me and say, "Angi, it's 9 o'clock. Isn't it past your curfew?"

Now when it's time for me to go home I get happy, because I know when I get home I'm not gonna be bored. I have a little brother to play with and I always wanted one. My little brother Zack is Mr. and Mrs. Cooper's biological son.

I never thought someone would read my story and help me move to a better home. Although I never expected it, my life did change by writing about it. Now I live with a family that cares about me and loves me and accepts me for who I am.

Angi was 16 when she wrote this story.

Kaite Martin

I'm Not Safe Here

By Tamara Scretching

Foster care exists to keep kids safe, but sometimes kids who are removed from their homes wind up in an abusive foster home or group home.

Children's Rights, an organization that advocates for kids in foster care, filed a lawsuit against the state of Oklahoma for failing to protect children from abuse while they were in state custody.

And although Oklahoma has one of the highest rates of reported foster care abuse in the country, it's not alone. The federal government sets a goal for states that says the rate of mistreatment of kids in foster care shouldn't be higher than 0.38%. Less than half of states met that standard. Three states—New York, Oklahoma, and Rhode Island—had abuse rates three times higher than the standard.

To learn more about the problem, I spoke to Julie Farber, director of policy at Children's Rights. At first, those abuse rates didn't seem very high to me, but after she explained it in numbers I was shocked.

"To put it in real terms," she explained, "on any given day in New York City you have 17,000 children in foster care. If 1% or more of them are being abused, that's 170 kids."

And that's only the cases that get reported. If the experiences of the writers here at Youth Communication are any indication, the actual rate of abuse in foster care is much higher.

So what can be done? Farber suggested things like better screening for people who want to become foster parents, regular home visits and check-ups from social workers, and better supervision for all caseworkers so that they take the right kind of action when they suspect abuse.

Social workers need to pay closer attention to what goes on in foster homes.

Farber also thinks social workers' case loads should be lowered so that they can build a better relationship with the teen and know if something is going on.

"In so many places the case loads are really high, and workers who have 60 cases are not going to be as responsive as they need to be," she said.

When I thought about my own situation, I realized social workers really do need to pay closer attention to what goes on in foster homes. In the past nine or 10 months, I've had three different social workers. And in the past four months, I only remember seeing my social worker twice. Every time she scheduled an appointment, she would show up hours after the scheduled time and then only stay for a few minutes.

Only one of these three social workers asked me if I felt safe in my environment. When I try to contact them, I get voice mail. Rarely have they ever called me back. If there was something going on in my foster home, how would my social worker even know?

Your social worker should be making sure that you're safe in your foster home, but unfortunately, it doesn't always happen that way. So if you are living in an abusive situation, let someone know.

Farber recommends that you talk to your lawyer, because that's the person who is legally responsible for representing you and advocating for your interests.

Even if you're not being abused, it's a good idea to ask your lawyer what to do if you ever do find yourself in this kind of situation. And having regular contact with your lawyer and caseworker gives you a better chance that someone will notice if something isn't right with your living situation, Farber said. She suggests trying to speak with these people often so that they get to know you.

If you're being abused and your lawyer or social worker isn't responding, call their supervisor. Or talk to another adult you trust, like a teacher, coach, or therapist. And if you don't get help from the first person you reach out to, keep talking until someone hears you.

If you are being abused or know someone who is, the National Child Abuse Hotline can connect you with sources of help in your community. Call 1-800-4-A-CHILD.

Tamara was 16 when she wrote this story.

Joseph Perez

My Foster Mom Is Mad Cool!

By Monique Martin

I know that when most kids go to a new home in the foster care system, they think the worst. Things run through your mind like, "What is this place going to be like? What kind of people will I meet?"

You always think the worst because you just don't know who to trust. I went through a similar situation myself.

When the social worker at my group home told me that I was going to be moving, I immediately got scared. I was only 13 and didn't know what to think. I had been at a diagnostic group home for almost two years. During my stay, I had made a lot of friends whom I considered to be my family.

I was not ready to move and start my life over when I had made a good one right there. What made me really pissed is that my social worker didn't even give me a week's notice so I could be prepared for the heartbreak that was coming. She only gave me two days. She explained that I had to go as soon as the placement was ready or I would lose my bed.

They were sending me to a foster home that happened to be in my old neighborhood. I wasn't mad anymore when I heard that. The staff and the residents gave me a party, and we all had a really good time.

The next day, I left. Ms. Lee, one of the staff, drove me over to my new agency. I wasn't thinking about my new foster mother or what her foster children were going to be like. Until...

I got into a taxi with my new social worker. That is when it all hit me. I was actually going to have to deal with these new people. What if there was a guy living in there? (I wouldn't feel comfortable undressing if there was.) What was I going to do if the new foster family didn't like me?

When my social worker told me I was moving, I immediately got scared.

My stomach began to tighten up as the car approached the white house where I would be staying. It was on a peaceful block, and the house looked like a castle. I had never lived in a private house before, only apartment buildings.

When Ms. Yvonne came to the door, for some reason my mind eased. She gave me a warm smile as our eyes connected and we said hello to each other. She was about 5'5" and African-American, with a smooth, deep brown complexion and glasses covering her dark brown eyes.

Inside, the house looked like a garden. There were nice big plants and sun shone through the window, which made the house seem even more beautiful than it already was.

I could see that Ms. Yvonne was paralyzed on one side. She explained to me that she had a stroke but did not need a wheelchair. She then told me a little more about herself.

Then she did something that a lot of people don't do. She asked me about myself. Yeah, she probably already looked at the little summary that the agency gives, but she let me tell the story that I wanted to tell.

I told her about my group home life, why I was in the system, and that I smoked cigarettes. She was very understanding about that.

I immediately felt a bond growing between me and my new foster mom. At first I didn't know how much I could trust her, but that was only for a quick minute.

The first month I was there, I mostly stayed in my room. Ms. Yvonne would come talk to me and ask me what the problem was. I would just lie on my bed for a few minutes and then answer, "Nothing."

Ms. Yvonne didn't handle the fact that I was being anti-social by screaming at me, nor did she play me in front of everybody. She actually took the time to ask me what I was feeling.

It felt really good to know that someone actually took the time to ask me, in a positive way, what was bothering me. I decided that maybe I should start socializing with everyone else in the house.

Another time when I went into one of my mood swings, I found out more about the lady I was living with. You see, I go into these little phases when I feel like I want to just go to another world so I don't have to deal with this one.

That is exactly what I was feeling about two months into my stay. I left the house to go to church one Sunday morning, and didn't tell anyone where I was going.

When I came back sometime later, Ms. Yvonne was in the living room watching television. She didn't say she was mad at me, but I sure felt it. Without jumping down my throat, she explained to me that I cannot do things like that. She said she knows I like to be alone but that is kind of hard to do because I am not the only one in the house.

I cried that day, not because she hurt my feelings but because I knew she was right. Also because she took the time out to listen to me. She asked me to tell her what was going on. One thing I liked was that she didn't cut me off when I was talking.

Ms. Yvonne helped me see a lot of things about myself that I never knew or cared about, such as my nonchalant attitude. For example:

"Monique, what is the attitude for?"

"I don't have an attitude."

"You've been walking around this house for three days with one."

For the rest of the conversation, I would just stand there not realizing that I was getting an attitude right in the middle of the conversation. I would never have known I did this if not for her. This is how our relationship really grew.

Ms. Yvonne is mad cool! Whatever you want to talk about, she is always there to give you advice and tell you what she thinks. If I want to talk to her about a boy I like, she doesn't say, "You don't need boyfriends now." If I want to talk to her about my mom, she gives me her opinion as a friend, not as another mom.

Then she did something that a lot of people don't do. She asked me about myself.

I remember when I had to register for school, she told me that it was up to me to go to school and that she wasn't going to be down my back. That showed me that she trusted me. She didn't just assume I was going to cut school.

I see Ms. Yvonne like a second mom, because she can deal with my mood swings and treat me like a human being.

Even though she has a daughter of her own, plus three other foster children (my sisters), she still finds a way to make each of us feel special and loved. If one wants something different to eat, she will try to make that dish for her. If one of us does something wrong, she doesn't immediately blame one person, she talks to everyone.

I don't know if Ms. Yvonne knows this, but I am grateful for what you have done for me. You will always have a special place in my heart. I love you, and I probably would have gone back to my old ways of cutting school and not caring if it weren't for you.

I hope I never have to leave your house, because I have finally found a place I can call my home. Thanks, Ma!

Monique was 15 when she wrote this story.

Rosheed Wellington

A Hi-Bye Relationship

By Cynthia Orbes

When I first stepped into my foster mother's house, I thought she was rich. The house looked so pretty. In the living room she had a big gold chandelier and gold tables and couches with plastic on them.

I was only 10 years old so I asked her, "Are you rich?" She said, "That is not something to ask somebody."

Although my foster mother's name is Aggie, everyone calls her Ms. Molly. She looks like she's in her early 30s so I was surprised to find out that she is about 50. Ms. Molly is laid back. She likes plants and designing her house, and most days she wears jeans and t-shirts. On Sunday she does her hair in curls and wears dresses to church.

Her husband's name is John but we call him Mr. J. He is quiet and calm, tall, and very light skinned. Mr. J. is a psychologist and works till late evening. I don't get to see him too often, but when I'm doing the dishes or eating in the kitchen and he comes downstairs after work, he asks me questions like, "Do you believe in God, Cynthia?" and, "How come you always wear black?" He's trying to figure me out.

When my sister and I first arrived at Ms. Molly and Mr. J's house, I felt abandoned. My mother had died of a heart attack that morning. My father had died two years before and my grandmother had died one year before, so my sister and I were all alone. Police took us to the precinct and then to a shelter where kids wait until they get a foster home. That night, all of a sudden, I was put with strangers.

I had believed that foster homes were horrible, dirty places that felt like jail, but Ms. Molly's house felt welcoming. Five other foster children were eating in Ms. Molly's kitchen when we got there. One of the foster kids, Barbara, showed us our beds and where to put our stuff. She was really nice.

The house was huge—a big brownstone with four floors and a basement. My sister and I had our own floor. The size made me feel kind of free. I could eat by myself or with my sister in the kitchen, or we could go to the backyard for air, or just sit on the stoop out front.

I would have liked it if my foster mom asked, "What's going on with you?" or, "How are you feeling?"

As nice as it was, moving to Ms. Molly's was a big change. I was forced to adapt to a new way of living. There are always so many kids eating together, watching TV, doing homework, and washing their clothes. Usually seven kids are living in Ms. Molly's house, and since I've been there at least 30 different kids have come through.

At first, I thought I couldn't get used to living with so many other kids. I was used to more privacy. I felt comfortable only with my sister and would follow her around the house everywhere she went until she became upset with me for doing so.

For a little while, adjusting to all the changes made me forget my mother and I was not too sad. Then, a month after I got there, I was watching a show on television and I closed my eyes and pretended that I was home. When I opened my eyes again I was still in the foster home. Finally, I let myself remember that my mother had died. I didn't want to believe it, but it hit me that it was true.

My sister saw me looking sad but I wanted to be alone so I ran downstairs and opened the door to the street. I heard my sister running after me. "What happened, Cynthia?" she said.

Ms. Molly told me to come to her. She told me to be strong. "Your mother is not in pain anymore, she is gone, and there is nothing you can do about it," she said. Then she gave me a peppermint and I went upstairs feeling calmer. I thought that my foster mother must have gone through what I was feeling, too.

After a few months, my sister and I were finally allowed to go home to get more of our stuff. I wanted very badly to go back to my old apartment, but when we got home we were overwhelmed. We didn't know what to take with us.

We looked for our family's photo album and my mother's old chest filled with foreign coins, cuff links, and a set of false teeth. She said it was my grandfather's chest and I wanted to hold on to it. But I never did find it that day. My sister and I rushed through packing up our stuff, because we felt sad and didn't want to think about old memories.

Over the years, I've adjusted to living with Ms. Molly and Mr. J., but they haven't become like family to me. We don't talk too much, only about my chores, curfew, allowance, and cleaning my room.

I try to stay out of the house after school because hanging out, talking to my friends, and reading at the library stop me from thinking about my mother. Especially in the first few years I'd stay out late, because going back to my foster home would remind me of why I was traveling to that destination in the first place.

My foster mother didn't understand why I was coming home late. She'd say, "Why were you late?" and I would just tell her that I was hanging out. Then she would yell. She probably thought that I just wanted to be rebellious.

I would have liked it if she asked, "What's going on with you?" or, "How are you feeling?" but I don't think she would have believed me if I told her the truth.

If I had any problems a girl might turn to her mother about—like boys or going through puberty—I talked to my sister, because we're close. With Ms. Molly, I'm just polite. If I see her before I go to sleep I say, "Good night," and when she wakes me up I say, "Good morning."

When I come home she usually says, "Hey, what's up?" Sometimes she tells me what's for dinner downstairs, or about something exciting that happened during the day, like she got something on sale. Sometimes I tell her about my day and sometimes I don't. If I'm upset about something, I keep it to myself.

The way I see it, a foster mother is not a mother.

Ms. Molly has never acted motherly to me, but I'm glad she's not very involved my life. I like having my space. The way I see it, a foster mother is not a mother.

When my mom was alive she showed me affection, and when we talked about funny stuff she would laugh. Sometimes we would have tickle fights, and many times she would read to me and help me with my homework.

My mother wanted me to do well, so she did my hair and helped dress me, she made sure that I went to school every day, and she cooked for me at night. She was special, and I don't want anyone to try to do the things that she did for me. My mom was the one who raised me, and she should get the credit.

My foster mother doesn't show that kind of affection to me and I don't expect her to. Sometimes I wonder, "Is my relationship with Ms. Molly wrong, weird, or OK?" I think it's OK for me.

When I'm 18 I plan to leave Ms. Molly's house and move into an apartment program. I think I will still keep in touch with Ms. Molly once I leave the house. I don't believe I'll need to depend on her, but I do hope that if I need her in some way, she will be there for me.

Cynthia was 17 when she wrote this story.
She later attended John Jay College.

Julio Juarez

Why I'll Be a Foster Mother

By Tamara Ballard

Have you ever moved around the foster care system and wished it was different? Did you ever wish that you could change the way some foster parents act? Have you ever complained about a foster parent and instead of the parent getting better training, you got moved?

Well, those things have all happened to me. It took me a while to realize that the way some foster parents act just doesn't change. It's like my sister said, "The system is the state's way of baby-sitting the kids who don't have parents that can take care of them."

As I look back on my complaints about foster parents, I realize that there's nothing I could have done to change their ways. For example, I once had a foster parent who would not let us in the kitchen after 9 p.m. If a foster child came in after 9 o'clock, even if she hadn't eaten, she still would not be allowed into the kitchen. The foster parent's mind was set that she was doing the right thing.

With other foster parents, there was no such thing as confidential when it came to their relationship with the foster child. That is why I really don't talk to my foster parents about real personal stuff, like about some of the boys in my life.

Also, they thought "who was I" to tell them what was wrong with the way they were treating me or one of the other kids. Some foster parents like to compare one foster child to another, or even to their own biological child. That's how some foster parents get on my bad side. In their eyes, I'm just a "minor with problems."

Recently, as I thought about my experiences as a foster child and listened to the stories of my peers and friends, I realized what I want to be when I get older.

This "minor with problems" has learned from her experiences with foster parents and it helped me make a decision: I want to become a foster parent. I decided this when I went through an emotional crisis and nobody was there for me. I want to be there for other kids. I know that many other teenagers go through what I've gone through. I think they could use advice from a "been there, done that" perspective.

Some foster parents are too wrapped up in their own lives to realize we need help. I plan on setting aside time to speak privately with my foster child. No matter how busy I get, I'll still make time. I'll set aside a good hour or so for each child—biological, foster, and adopted. Sometimes we'll talk as a group, but other times I'll talk to them individually.

Some foster parents take the clothing allowance and the money they're paid and spend it on themselves. When I was in kinship, I didn't even know I was getting clothing allowance until one day my caseworker told me. I then began to wonder: if my aunt is getting money to buy me clothes, why was I wearing hand-me-downs from her daughter's friends?

I plan on taking my foster child shopping for clothes and spending all of her check on her. I won't be afraid to take money out of my own pocket to buy other necessities, instead of depending only on the check.

Some foster parents tend to treat foster kids as if they are a contagious virus. Although we are normal kids, they take the label "foster" and run with it. They do things like give us different eating utensils, or tell us to heat up leftovers while their biological kids are eating out.

I plan to treat my foster children the same as my own biological children. We will eat together as a family and everyone will have the same kind of food. Occasionally we will all eat out as a family.

Some foster parents don't realize verbal abuse can affect a child for the rest of her life. For

Little signs of caring can make life more livable for the foster child.

example, I would not keep reminding foster children that they are in the system. I also would not let the biological children who live in the house remind them.

One of my younger foster sisters likes to remind me of that fact. It is one of my soft spots and she knows it. I think that is total disrespect on her part. The foster child already knows she is in the system and does not need to be reminded. She needs to learn to accept that fact and get on with her life.

I want a foster kid to have a more positive experience than I did. I would compliment and reprimand the child as if she was my own.

It's not always what a foster mother does or says that hurts, but, in some cases, what she doesn't. Little signs of caring can make life more livable for the foster child. There needs to be more communication. Some foster parents just have to give a little and so can the foster kids. It's just pride keeping both foster parents and youth from admitting they are wrong and making a change for the better.

If the setting in the house was more family-like, a foster child could feel more comfortable admitting when she's wrong. The foster child might even open up a little more.

As for the foster parents, they are older—they should know how to put their pride aside when it comes to those important issues.

I've had some good foster parents. They had their bad spots, but all in all they were good. With my present foster mother, every so often I feel comfortable enough to sit down with her and have an actual conversation (I mostly talk to my foster sister). My foster mother is one of my role models.

I admit when I first moved in I had doubts about her. After two bad foster homes and two temporary homes, I thought she was going to be short-term just like the rest. Without knowing her personally, I categorized her with the title "foster mother." But after a while I stopped stereotyping her and I realized she was trying to help me, not hurt me.

My foster mom is adjusting to my ways, and at the same time I'm learning to trust her.

If I have an attitude, she leaves me alone. When I want to talk, she makes the time. She is adjusting to my ways, and at the same time I'm learning to trust her. Last summer I tried to commit suicide. My foster mother was there for me, from the time I entered the hospital until the time I was discharged. She could have gotten rid of me, using the excuse that I would be too much trouble, but she didn't. In September I started calling her "Mommy," because that is who she is to me now.

Even though I've had many bad experiences in foster care, I still want to become a foster mother. I realize how hard it is to raise a child. Whether the child is biological or foster, young or old, she's still going to give grief.

Back in the day, a child was more respectful to her parents and other adults. Nowadays some children disrespect everyone, from their own parents to complete strangers. I realize how stressful it might be, but I still want to become a foster parent. I don't make promises I can't keep.

Tamara was 16 when she wrote this story.
She now lives in Georgia.

Qing Zhiang

My Place in the World

By Fannie Harris

Last year, a supervisor at my foster care agency suggested I speak on a panel about the experiences of kids in care. In the hallway, I noticed a woman with short gray hair wearing a rainbow watch. Her name was Mary Keane. She pulled me aside and asked me to speak on a panel she was hosting on "Being Different."

I've always been different from other kids because I'm black but prefer rock and roll to r&b and rap. So I wasn't surprised that she asked me.

Then Mary asked me if I was gay. Unlike the kids who ask me that on the bus, Mary didn't seem to be asking so she could make fun of me or so she could say something vulgar or rude. I didn't know what to tell her. I said I thought I was straight but that I wasn't sure.

Even though I've always felt different and have been attracted to girls as far back as I can remember, I resisted accepting that part of myself because I didn't want to be gay. Admitting that I might be gay scared me because when I was little another girl tried to molest me. And once, when I was 5, I saw my mom having sex and it felt strange and upsetting to me.

*E*ven so, it was finally dawning on me that I was gay. A few months before, I had gone to the gay pride parade in Greenwich Village in New York City with some friends. I went just for fun (I had never been to the Village before, which is a neighborhood where a lot of gay people live).

The scene was wild and crazy and I loved it. I never knew the gay community was so large and filled with so many different people. A voice inside my head said, "The time to realize my sexuality is now!" After the parade, I thought that there could be no other place in the world where I could fit in and say, "This is me, this is who I am." It turned out I was wrong.

Then Mary asked me if I was gay. I wasn't entirely sure what to tell her.

At the panel, Mary told me she was an open lesbian and it didn't bother me because she seemed so normal. Then I met some of Mary's foster kids and soon went to visit them at Mary's house.

The house was huge! It had four floors, 11 bedrooms (some of which aren't even used), six bathrooms, a library, and three living rooms. She had seven kids in the house and there were gay rainbow flags all over the place.

All the kids living there said, "This is the best place I've ever been in." At the time I hated my foster home. My foster mother made me do almost all the cleaning, so I felt like Cinderella. She picked favorites and treated her biological daughter better than me. I wanted to leave there because she made me so stressed out that I cried myself to sleep almost every night. The more I visited Mary's, the more comfortable I felt. "Oh my God, this is my haven," I thought. My inhibitions about gay people started to fall away.

I moved into Mary's house in November. That is when I found a place where I could be my best self, my true self. It felt like living my destiny. About a month after arriving, I stopped caring about what other people thought of my sexuality. I was left with a decision to make—what was my sexuality going to be?

For a while I maintained the straight gig. I didn't quite want to label myself as gay, even though, in my heart, I knew there was a deep reason why I felt so comfortable in this new place.

Mary didn't flaunt her sexuality, so she didn't really influence me in coming out. But the kids...they helped me hit the nail on the head. The kids mainly hung out in the basement, where there's a television. One day a Jennifer Lopez video came on and one of the girls said something complimentary about her rear end. In my head, I found myself agreeing. "OK, there, I made up my mind," I thought. "Telling everybody else is going to be the hard part."

Amanda, a friend of my foster brother and sister, often spent the night at the house. Sometimes I don't notice even obvious things, so when my foster sister told me that Amanda liked me, my reaction was, "Stop lying!" and, "She doesn't even act like she's attracted to me!"

But one night after a party, Amanda handed me a letter telling me that she liked me. She also wrote that it was OK if I wasn't gay, but that she hoped we could at least become good friends. That threw me off. I was shocked and afraid because I didn't know if she was serious or just playing around.

I didn't want to get caught in a love jones that turned out to be a hoax. But the more I got to know her, the more I realized that she was trustworthy. My feelings for her started to grow and grow.

It took about two or three months of continuous letter writing before we actually got to the point where we both understood that we were going to go out. We were pretty much writing about little third grade things like how our day went and how we felt about one another. She was the first girl that I'd ever gone out with.

Dates with Amanda don't really happen much because we're both really busy, but when we do get to spend time with each other it's usually at her house or going to the movies. At first I was a little weirded out by the fact that I was going to be seen holding hands with a girl. But I've had to adjust to a lot of different scenarios in my life, and it only took about a month to get both myself and everyone else used to my relationship with Amanda.

Moving in with a gay parent has given me a positive outlook on what being homosexual is all about.

We express affection toward each other in the same way that any couple would: hugging, holding hands, kissing, and all such. Being with her feels right because my mind and heart say so and I agree with them both.

Moving in with a gay parent has given me a positive outlook on what being homosexual is all about. It's not so much because Mary is gay, but just because of the kind of person she is. You'd have to know her to understand the feeling for yourself.

Mary seems like she's been around since the world began, and when you talk to her it seems like she has the answers to everything. She's also able to handle both parental roles and control all the kids with no problem. She's a role model to me.

So far I've chosen not to talk to Mary about my sexuality, because seeing me with Amanda she already knows. I also don't think it really matters. But I know that, if I ever needed to, I could go up to Mary and tell her something about girl problems and not have to worry if she's going to judge me or ridicule what I'm telling her. I don't have to worry that Mary would take me to church to try to get this "demon" out of me.

I'm emotionally and physically stable in my current situation, and I'm much happier now that I don't have to wake up every morning wondering what sexual orientation I have to pretend to be to please everybody else. Staying at Mary's house reminds me of being at the parade. I'm finally at a place where I belong.

Fannie was 16 when she wrote this story.

Martell Brown

Learning to Love Again

By Aquellah Mahdi

The first time Yolanda saw my twin sister Taheerah and me, we were cursing out our foster parent. Yolanda was going to be our next foster mom. Who knows what she had in her head about us. We were new to the agency, so the only things in our file were bad things: that we violated curfew and didn't do our chores, that I smoked and that my sister drank.

I believed she thought, "As soon as they act up once they're out of my home." That was the kind of attitude my sister and I had encountered at the other homes we'd been in.

Taheerah and I entered care four years ago, after we spoke up about our father's abuse. The first year we lived with five different foster families.

We lived with a woman who only seemed to care about how much money she was going to get for us. Another foster mother's main concern was that we wouldn't say anything bad about her home, which was sweet on the outside but salty on the inside. Those bad experiences made me think all foster moms were the same. I couldn't imagine trusting any of them.

It was a relief when we were placed in a group home, but it hurt not to have anyone looking out for us. We ran free like little animals without an owner to watch us. Three years later, our group home was closed, and we went back to bouncing from one foster home to another.

At the agency a few days before we moved into her home, the only thing Yolanda said was, "There are chores and a curfew." I didn't know what to think of her, only that she was going to be my next victim. I was going to try to hurt her before she got rid of my sister and me. I thought it would be better to get kicked out for bad behavior than to have her reject us.

We walked into Yolanda's home feeling sure that within the next month or two we would be on our way out.

My sister and I walked into Yolanda's home feeling sure that within the next month or two we would be on our way out. There was no need to get all attached to the room, the bed, or even the rules.

But that first day at Yolanda's home my rabbit died. I started to cry. That rabbit was so small and defenseless. It needed me and I let it die. Then Yolanda hugged me. "If that happened to my cat Jackie, I would feel the same way that you do," she said. She wanted my rabbit to be buried and offered to buy me another one. That's how I realized she wasn't a fake.

I felt different at that moment. It was like she felt the anger that I had inside of me, and was saying that it was OK to feel that way. That it was OK to be sad and for me to let my guard down, that not everyone in the world was out to harm me or my sister. That it was OK to let someone into my world and let them help me. It was just a hug, but it meant so much.

As the months passed, I began to feel a little bit more at ease. But memories of my past started to rise to the surface. I started having a lot of bad dreams about my dad, and I got so confused and scared.

One day when I was feeling depressed, I told Yolanda I was feeling sad. She said, "Why do you think that you're sad?"

"I don't know," I replied. "I just do." Then I looked at her and we just sat there and laughed. It was like we both knew that I wanted to talk but I wasn't ready to let it all out. She didn't push me. Instead she told me, "When you're ready to talk, text me on my cell phone." That was fine with me. I liked that.

When I told her about my nightmares, Yolanda stayed with me in my room and tried to comfort me. I talked to her a little, but I couldn't get it all out so she just let me know that she was there for me.

"Any time you need me, come and knock on my door," she said, unlike other foster moms who just called 911 to have someone come and get me. When she left I was still a little bit scared, but more at ease.

Sometimes I talked to her about my dad, and how I was scared that he was going to come back and kill me, or how sometimes I could just feel him touching me, even though the abuse stopped years ago.

Sometimes I'd feel like Yolanda, Taheerah, and even our foster sisters had vanished from me, like the night had devoured them and left me alone. I started staying up late so that I could beat whatever might come and try to hurt my new family. I kept a knife to protect us.

Yolanda had to take that away from me. When she did, she reassured me that she would never let anything happen to my sister or me. For some reason I believed her, I guess because she didn't seem to mind that she had to be there for me in the night. Or if she did, she had the perfect way of hiding it so that I didn't feel like I was bothering her.

Then, in November, my sister signed herself into a psychiatric hospital because she was feeling depressed. When I saw her at school, she was going to therapy and I was going home. That afternoon Yolanda got a phone call from someone at the agency. Taheerah was on her way to a hospital upstate. I couldn't believe it.

"Your sister cut herself," Yolanda told me.

"Is she really going to the hospital?"

"Yes, that is what I was told."

I rushed to the phone to call my law guardian to get Taheerah out, but I couldn't get in contact with her. It didn't occur to me until later that Taheerah wanted to be in the hospital.

When I told her about my nightmares, Yolanda stayed with me in my room and tried to comfort me.

That still didn't stop me from becoming stressed out. For months, I pretty much stopped eating. Yolanda was there with me during everything.

"Aquellah, I know that you are stressed but you have to eat or you will get so sick," she told me.

"I miss her, I want my sister."

"I don't know why she wanted to hurt herself like that," Yolanda told me, "but I guess that she needed help and she is going to get it now at the hospital." She hugged me and I just stayed like that, crying on her shoulder for a little while.

A few nights after that I woke up in a panic. I couldn't stay asleep. Yolanda came into my room. "Aquellah, what's wrong?" I couldn't even tell her how I felt. I couldn't get the words out to say what was the matter.

"Aquellah, you're safe here, OK? If anyone tries to get through the door to hurt you, I will get them." I was glad that she was so aggressive—it made me feel like I could loosen up and let someone else protect me. I didn't have to worry anymore.

I'm grateful to have Yolanda as a foster parent, because in a way she is more than just a foster parent—she's a lifesaver. When she tells me (and sometimes she has to tell me this over and over), "You have to stop being the victim," I don't mind. She wants to go with me on my journeys and help me find my way back home, to her home.

I would love to stay with Yolanda until I age out. She has accepted me, my sister, and all the baggage we brought to her home. Instead of pushing us away, she's taught herself how to help us deal with our problems, and whatever we might face in the future.

Aquellah was 19 when she wrote this story.
She attended Lehman College.

Amaury Almonte / YC Art Dept.

Take It Slow: How to Get to Know a New Family

Cori Herzig, a therapist in Santa Rosa, California, explains some good techniques for adjusting to a new family—and how you know when it's just not working out.

Q: How can you get to know a new foster family?

A: A major part of adjusting to a family is learning their routine. Not just how they wash the dishes or when they eat, but how open they are and what's OK to say around them. Learn when you can be more relaxed and what are signs you should keep your mouth shut. You know with your own family: "When dad comes in with that look on his face, I'm not going to bring up that I need money." Or, "When mom is stirring her coffee a certain way, she's stressed."

Noticing when is a good time to talk and when isn't will help you get the response you want when you open up. If you open up at the wrong moment, you risk a feeling of rejection which can snowball into feeling misunderstood.

You can also remember that it's a typical thing for teens to feel misunderstood by their families. Teens have so much going on inside, and all teens wonder, "What's my place?" Add to that having to adjust to a foster home, and it's going to be hard to figure out what's what.

Q: How do you know if you're trusting too much or not enough?

A: When I was young, my mother became a foster parent to teenage girls. Some would come in and call her "mom" immediately and tell their life story to everyone in the household. Other girls that had been burned in their last placement

Sometimes kids come into a home almost daring the family to reject them.

or family of origin weren't going to tell anybody anything. If you're at one of those extremes, it's going to be harder for you to get close to people.

If you're opening up too quickly, you might feel overexposed or vulnerable, or you might be overwhelming others. Paying attention to your own body signals, in particular your breathing, can help. If you're talking really fast and breathing shallow, you might be talking out of fear, not a desire to be known. You can always slow down, breathe, and trust yourself to go at a slower pace.

On the other end, if you hear people telling you, "It's hard to get to know you," or you feel apart from the family, you might want to try opening up more. The desire to be known is a healthy one.

Q: What are some signs that this isn't a good placement for you?

A: There are some obvious signs, like somebody is being verbally or physically abusive, or neglectful. Those are clearly not OK.

If you are making efforts to get to know people and you keep trying to communicate and work on it, and you keep feeling criticized or like you're in a hole and feeling like, "No matter what I do I can't get these people to like me," I don't think you should stay in that situation. Talk to your social worker and say, "I've been trying." Tell the social worker everything you've tried, and say, "This isn't working. This feels bad for me."

But sometimes kids move from home to home because they come into a home almost daring the family to reject them, saying, "I don't have to adapt to you for me to belong. It's not fair." That anger is understandable, but if it becomes a central part of your identity that you won't adapt and you must be heard, it's going to be painful for you to try to connect to people even after you're out of foster care.

Patricia Battles

The First Good Christmas

By Aquellah Mahdi

Even as a young child at home with my family, I never had a good Christmas. I was told we were Muslims so we didn't celebrate Christmas. But we didn't celebrate anything else, either.

When I came home from school with a toy from Santa Claus one year, my aunt said, "Christmas is a lie! No wishes come true, especially not for naughty kids like you." That's when it came to my attention that Christmas must be a fairy tale. I think that's when the hopes my sister and I had for a true Christmas were smashed.

We had believed that Christmas was supposed to be a time when you got a lot of nice things from your loved ones and sat around a big tree decorated with gifts, or even like a Christmas on TV where something wicked happens but good prevails. But our aunt let us know that wasn't for us. She acted like we were dirt, like we didn't matter. As I got older this was the reason the holidays seemed like days of torture.

In the last four years, my sister Taheerah and I have been in 11 foster homes and three group homes. We were always in a new home around the holidays. We were unexpected guests in people's homes, and they never had time to buy us anything.

I would tell my sister "Merry Christmas," or we would just try to forget about it. We did try to buy each other gifts, but we had hardly any money. We would buy a lot of cookies, ice cream, and cakes, and blame ourselves for telling about the abuse that put us in foster care. After all, if we hadn't talked we wouldn't be alone watching TV for the holidays. We had no one but each other, and occasionally that was not enough.

Over the holidays, we'd be sitting in the group homes or foster homes with different people walking in and out, looking at us like we were some kind of disease. It was hard. Many of the kids in our group home had someone to come get them, but my sister and I had no one. All we could do was just stare out our window and wonder what it would be like to wake up on Christmas morning with gifts, hugs, and smiles from everyone.

I imagined a big breakfast with eggs, bacon, pancakes, waffles, and fresh juice. The fantasy was so real. I could just smell the aroma, but then I would hear a voice: "Aquellah, wake up, come get breakfast. It's cereal." My dream was over. Just like that I had to wake up and face the real world.

I remember one group home in particular that treated us on Christmas like we did not mean anything to anyone. The staff cooked the little we had in the house for our dinner and made rude comments about how they had better food at home, which made me mad.

On Christmas day, each girl was given a sweater. Only a sweater! Taheerah and I were given the same damn color—purple—and the staff's excuse was, "It's because you're twins." Those purple things were hideous—they were big and made you look like Barney or an old grandmother who sits all day knitting those sweaters.

The girls got so mad that they started cursing, mainly because they had all written wish lists and were hoping to be getting at least one item from the list.

"I hate this insulting house. You people treat us like animals! All we get is a damn sweater!" one of the girls yelled.

"Calm down or I will call the police!" the staff yelled back. "I'm going to write you up. Don't make me go and get my book!"

That night, many of the girls violated curfew or ran back to their abusive parents' homes. On Christmas you just don't want to be alone, insulted, or feel like you don't have family.

My sister and I were thinking about going home to see our family, too, but we had to stop and think of what could happen

I worried that if she was that strict, she wouldn't accept me as I was.

if we did. We wanted so much to have a safe place to go home to, but we really didn't have that.

Our dad could abuse us physically and our mother could abuse us emotionally with her accusations about how we broke down a happy home. Our siblings could just reject us. We hadn't seen our brothers that entire year and our mother had brainwashed them to believe that my sister and I were either crazy or just wanted all of us kids to be taken away for no reason.

We came to the conclusion that it was for the best that we stayed put. We had nowhere else to go, no home but the group home.

The following year we were blessed to be placed in a foster home with Yolanda Crosby, who I call Precious because she is just phenomenal. But when we first came to her home I thought I'd be out of there in about two months. I was doubtful about her rules.

Yolanda made me do different chores, like cleaning the bathroom, kitchen, and living room. Then she'd be on my back about my education.

I worried that if she was that strict, she wouldn't accept me as I was. I didn't realize that having someone care about my education would make me want to do more to pass. I didn't realize that I would wake up to the Christmas that I'd wanted since I was a child.

Actually, as the days of December came, I got a little anxious. Yolanda was talking about presents, but I hadn't bought presents for people in years. I thought, "What if they don't like them?" I was scared. Yolanda never did tell me what to get her for Christmas. She just said, "I want to make sure everybody is happy."

I stopped feeling scared as the days got closer to Christmas. The tree was put up—white with colorful lights and ornaments. A music box under the tree played Christmas carols that I'd never really heard. As the hours counted down to the big day I'd waited for my whole life, I could only sit in front of the 87 gifts and imagine what was inside the ones that had my name on them.

On Christmas Eve, Yolanda allowed my foster sisters, Taheerah, and me to open one gift each before we went to bed. "Here Aquellah, this is yours," she said. It was a cute lingerie set. I had never really had my own gift before, without sharing it with my twin. I was so happy. I thanked her and gave her a hug. I felt like crying.

In the morning, Yolanda gave my sisters and me the rest of our gifts. We were so nervous we didn't want to tear the wrapping. Afterwards we all tried on our clothes like we were America's Next Top Models preparing for a series of photo shoots. We had bacon, eggs, and pancakes for breakfast—it was a feast made for a queen, I must say.

Then we went to Yolanda's mother's house for a big dinner. When I entered the hallway, the smell of turkey, ham, macaroni and cheese, and all kinds of pie filled the air. I couldn't believe it.

It smelled like my dream of home.

Inside it looked like Christmas with her white tree, just like Yolanda's, only the ornaments were red and blue. She greeted us with kisses and hugs. We all exchanged gifts and sat around to hear stories about Yolanda when she was a little girl. It was wonderful. It felt like something I'd missed, but was starting to learn.

That Christmas changed how I view the holiday. I didn't see it as another day for my sister and me to punish ourselves, but a time for us to be around people who care for us. It meant a new start.

Hopefully this Christmas will be as joyful and tranquil as the last. I believe that my wish came true. Santa Claus gave me a complete family for Christmas and blissful times to remember.

Aquellah was 21 when she wrote this story.
She attended Lehman College.

Lost and Found

Darcy Wills winced at the loud rap music coming from her sister's room.

> My rhymes were rockin'
> MC's were droppin'
> People shoutin' and hip-hoppin'
> Step to me and you'll be inferior
> 'Cause I'm your lyrical superior.

Darcy went to Grandma's room. The darkened room smelled of lilac perfume, Grandma's favorite, but since her stroke Grandma did not notice it, or much of anything.

"Bye, Grandma," Darcy whispered from the doorway. "I'm going to school now."

Just then, the music from Jamee's room cut off, and Jamee rushed into the hallway.

The teen characters in the Bluford novels, a fiction series by Townsend Press, struggle with many of the same difficult issues as the writers in this book. Here's the first chapter from *Lost and Found*, by Anne Schraff, the first book in the series. In this novel, high school sophomore Darcy contends with the return of her long-absent father, the troubling behavior of her younger sister Jamee, and the beginning of her first relationship.

"Like she even hears you," Jamee said as she passed Darcy. Just two years younger than Darcy, Jamee was in eighth grade, though she looked older.

"It's still nice to talk to her. Sometimes she understands. You want to pretend she's not here or something?"

"She's not," Jamee said, grabbing her backpack.

"Did you study for your math test?" Darcy asked. Mom was an emergency room nurse who worked rotating shifts. Most of the time, Mom was too tired to pay much attention to the girls' schoolwork. So Darcy tried to keep track of Jamee.

"Mind your own business," Jamee snapped.

"You got two D's on your last report card," Darcy scolded. "You wanna flunk?" Darcy did not want to sound like a nagging parent, but Jamee wasn't doing her best. Maybe she couldn't make A's like Darcy, but she could do better.

Jamee stomped out of the apartment, slamming the door behind her. "Mom's trying to get some rest!" Darcy yelled. "Do you have to be so selfish?" But Jamee was already gone, and the apartment was suddenly quiet.

Darcy loved her sister. Once, they had been good friends. But now all Jamee cared about was her new group of rowdy friends. They leaned on cars outside of school and turned up rap music on their boom boxes until the street seemed to tremble like an earthquake. Jamee had even stopped hanging out with her old friend Alisha Wrobel, something she used to do every weekend.

Darcy went back into the living room, where her mother sat in the recliner sipping coffee. "I'll be home at 2:30, Mom," Darcy said. Mom smiled faintly. She was tired, always tired. And lately she was worried too. The hospital where she worked was cutting staff. It seemed each day fewer people were expected to do more work. It was like trying to climb a mountain that keeps getting taller as you go. Mom was forty-four, but just yesterday she said, "I'm like an old car that's run out of warranty, baby. You know what happens then. Old car is ready for the junk heap. Well, maybe that hospital is gonna tell me one of these days—'Mattie Mae Wills, we don't need you anymore. We can get somebody younger and cheaper.'"

"Mom, you're not old at all," Darcy had said, but they were only words, empty words. They could not erase the dark, weary lines from beneath her mother's eyes.

Darcy headed down the street toward Bluford High School. It was not a terrible neighborhood they lived in; it just was not good. Many front yards were not cared for. Debris—fast food wrappers, plastic bags, old newspapers—blew around and piled against fences and curbs. Darcy hated that. Sometimes she and other kids from school spent Saturday mornings cleaning up, but it seemed a losing battle. Now, as she walked, she tried to focus on small spots of beauty along the way. Mrs. Walker's pink and white roses bobbed proudly in the morning breeze. The Hustons' rock garden was carefully designed around a wooden windmill.

As she neared Bluford, Darcy thought about the science project that her biology teacher, Ms. Reed, was assigning. Darcy was doing hers on tidal pools. She was looking forward to visiting a real tidal pool, taking pictures, and doing research. Today, Ms. Reed would be dividing the students into teams of two. Darcy wanted to be paired with her close friend, Brisana Meeks. They were both excellent students, a cut above most kids at Bluford, Darcy thought.

"Today, we are forming project teams so that each student can gain something valuable from the other," Ms. Reed said as Darcy sat at her desk. Ms. Reed was a tall, stately woman who reminded Darcy of the Statue of Liberty. She would have been a perfect model for the statue if Lady Liberty had been a black woman. She never would have been called pretty, but it was possible she might have been called a handsome woman. "For this assignment, each of you will be working with someone you've never worked with before."

Darcy was worried. If she was not teamed with Brisana,

maybe she would be teamed with some really dumb student who would pull her down. Darcy was a little ashamed of herself for thinking that way. Grandma used to say that all flowers are equal, but different. The simple daisy was just as lovely as the prize rose. But still Darcy did not want to be paired with some weak partner who would lower her grade.

"Darcy Wills will be teamed with Tarah Carson," Ms. Reed announced.

Darcy gasped. Not Tarah! Not that big, chunky girl with the brassy voice who squeezed herself into tight skirts and wore lime green or hot pink satin tops and cheap jewelry. Not Tarah who hung out with Cooper Hodden, that loser who was barely hanging on to his football eligibility. Darcy had heard that Cooper had been left back once or twice and even got his driver's license as a sophomore. Darcy's face felt hot with anger. Why was Ms. Reed doing this?

Hakeem Randall, a handsome, shy boy who sat in the back row, was teamed with the class blabbermouth, LaShawn Appleby. Darcy had a secret crush on Hakeem since freshman year. So far she had only shared this with her diary, never with another living soul.

It was almost as though Ms. Reed was playing some devilish game. Darcy glanced at Tarah, who was smiling broadly. Tarah had an enormous smile, and her teeth contrasted harshly with her dark red lipstick. "Great," Darcy muttered under her breath.

Ms. Reed ord e red the teams to meet so they could begin to plan their projects.

As she sat down by Tarah, Darcy was instantly sickened by a syrupy-sweet odor.

She must have doused herself with cheap perfume this morning , Darcy thought.

"Hey, girl," Tarah said. "Well, don't you look down in the mouth. What's got you lookin' that way?"

It was hard for Darcy to meet new people, especially someone like Tarah, a person Aunt Charlotte would call "low class." These were people who were loud and rude. They drank too much, used drugs, got into fights and ruined the neighborhood. They yelled ugly insults at people, even at their friends. Darcy did not actually know that Tarah did anything like this personally, but she seemed like the type who did.

"I just didn't think you'd be interested in tidal pools," Darcy explained.

Tarah slammed her big hand on the desk, making her gold bracelets jangle like ice cubes in a glass, and laughed. Darcy had never heard a mule bray, but she was sure it made exactly the same sound. Then Tarah leaned close and whispered, "Girl, I don't know a tidal pool from a fool. Ms. Reed stuck us together to mess with our heads, you hear what I'm sayin'?"

"Maybe we could switch to other partners," Darcy said nervously.

A big smile spread slowly over Tarah's face. "Nah, I think I'm gonna enjoy this. You're always sittin' here like a princess collecting your A's. Now you gotta work with a regular person, so you better loosen up, girl!"

Darcy felt as if her teeth were glued to her tongue. She fumbled in her bag for her outline of the project. It all seemed like a horrible joke now. She and Tarah Carson standing knee-deep in the muck of a tidal pool!

"Worms live there, don't they?" Tarah asked, twisting a big gold ring on her chubby finger.

"Yeah, I guess," Darcy replied.

"Big green worms," Tarah continued. "So if you get your feet stuck in the bottom of that old tidal pool, and you can't get out, do the worms crawl up your clothes?"

Darcy ignored the remark. "I'd like for us to go there soon, you know, look around."

"My boyfriend, Cooper, he goes down to the ocean all the time. He can take us. He says he's seen these fiddler crabs. They look like big spiders, and they'll try to bite your toes off. Cooper says so," Tarah said.

"Stop being silly," Darcy shot back. "If you' re not even going to be serious . . . "

"You think you're better than me, don't you?" Tarah suddenly growled.

"I never said—" Darcy blurted.

"You don't have to say it, girl. It's in your eyes. You think I'm a low-life and you're something special. Well, I got more friends than you got fingers and toes together. You got no friends, and everybody laughs at you behind your back. Know what the word on you is? Darcy Wills give you the chills."

Just then, the bell rang, and Darcy was glad for the excuse to turn away from Tarah, to hide the hot tears welling in her eyes. She quickly rushed from the classroom, relieved that school was over. Darcy did not think she could bear to sit through another class just now.

Darcy headed down the long street towards home. She did not like Tarah. Maybe it was wrong, but it was true. Still, Tarah's brutal words hurt. Even stupid, awful people might tell you the truth about yourself. And Darcy did not have any real friends, except for Brisana. Maybe the other kids were mocking her behind her back. Darcy was very slender, not as shapely as many of the other girls. She remembered the time when Cooper Hodden was hanging in front of the deli with his friends, and he yelled as Darcy went by, "Hey, is that really a female there? Sure don't look like it. Looks more like an old broomstick with hair. " His companions laughed rudely, and Darcy had walked a little faster.

A terrible thought clawed at Darcy. Maybe she was the loser, not Tarah. Tarah was always hanging with a bunch of kids, laughing and joking. She would go down the hall to the lockers and greetings would come from everywhere. "Hey, Tarah!" "What's up, Tar?" "See ya at lunch, girl." When Darcy went to the lockers, there was dead silence.

Darcy usually glanced into stores on her way home from school. She enjoyed looking at the trays of chicken feet and pork ears at the little Asian grocery store. Sometimes she would even steal a glance at the diners sitting by the picture window at the Golden Grill Restaurant. But today she stared straight ahead, her shoulders drooping.

If this had happened last year, she would have gone directly to Grandma's house, a block from where Darcy lived. How many times had Darcy and Jamee run to Grandma's, eaten applesauce cookies, drunk cider, and poured out their troubles to Grandma. Somehow, their problems would always dissolve in the warmth of her love and wisdom. But now Grandma was a frail figure in the corner of their apartment, saying little. And what little she did say made less and less sense.

Darcy was usually the first one home. The minute she got there, Mom left for the hospital to take the 3:00 to 11:00 shift in the ER. By the time Mom finished her paperwork at the hospital, she would be lucky to be home again by midnight. After Mom left, Darcy went to Grandma's room to give her the malted nutrition drink that the doctor ordered her to have three times a day.

"Want to drink your chocolate malt, Grandma?" Darcy asked, pulling up a chair beside Grandma's bed.

Grandma was sitting up, and her eyes were open. "No. I'm not hungry," she said listlessly. She always said that.

"You need to drink your malt, Grandma," Darcy insisted, gently putting the straw between the pinched lips.

Grandma sucked the malt slowly. "Grandma, nobody likes me at school," Darcy said. She did not expect any response. But there was a strange comfort in telling Grandma anyway. "Everybody laughs at me. It's because I'm shy and maybe stuck-up, too, I guess. But I don't mean to be. Stuck-up, I mean. Maybe I'm weird. I could be weird, I guess. I could be like Aunt Charlotte . . ." Tears rolled down Darcy's cheeks. Her heart ached with loneliness. There was nobody to talk to anymore, nobody who had time to listen, nobody who understood.

Grandma blinked and pushed the straw away. Her eyes brightened as they did now and then. "You are a wonderful girl. Everybody knows that," Grandma said in an almost normal voice. It happened like that sometimes. It was like being in the middle of a dark storm and having the clouds part, revealing a patch of clear, sunlit blue. For just a few precious minutes, Grandma was bright-eyed and saying normal things.

"Oh, Grandma, I'm so lonely," Darcy cried, pressing her head against Grandma's small shoulder.

"You were such a beautiful baby," Grandma said, stroking her hair." 'That one is going to shine like the morning star.' That's what I told your Mama. 'That child is going to shine like the morning star.' Tell me, Angelcake, is your daddy home yet?"

Darcy straightened. "Not yet." Her heart pounded so hard, she could feel it thumping in her chest. Darcy's father had not been home in five years.

"Well, tell him to see me when he gets home. I want him to buy you that blue dress you liked in the store window. That's for you, Angelcake. Tell him I've got money. My social security came, you know. I have money for the blue dress," Grandma said, her eyes slipping shut.

Just then, Darcy heard the apartment door slam. Jamee had come home. Now she stood in the hall, her hands belligerently on her hips. "Are you talking to Grandma again?" Jamee demanded.

"She was talking like normal," Darcy said. "Sometimes she does. You know she does."

"That is so stupid," Jamee snapped. "She never says anything right anymore. Not anything!" Jamee's voice trembled.

Darcy got up quickly and set down the can of malted milk. She ran to Jamee and put her arms around her sister. "Jamee, I know you're hurting too."

"Oh, don't be stupid," Jamee protested, but Darcy hugged her more tightly, and in a few seconds Jamee was crying. "She was the best thing in this stupid house," Jamee cried. "Why'd she have to go?"

"She didn't go," Darcy said. "Not really."

"She did! She did!" Jamee sobbed. She struggled free of Darcy, ran to her room, and slammed the door. In a minute, Darcy heard the bone-rattling sound of rap music.

Teens:
How to Get More Out of This Book

Self-help: The teens who wrote the stories in this book did so because they hope that telling their stories will help readers who are facing similar challenges. They want you to know that you are not alone, and that taking specific steps can help you manage or overcome very difficult situations. They've done their best to be clear about the actions that worked for them so you can see if they'll work for you.

Writing: You can also use the book to improve your writing skills. Each teen in this book wrote 5-10 drafts of his or her story before it was published. If you read the stories closely you'll see that the teens work to include a beginning, a middle, and an end, and good scenes, description, dialogue, and anecdotes (little stories). To improve your writing, take a look at how these writers construct their stories. Try some of their techniques in your own writing.

Reading: Finally, you'll notice that we include the first chapter from a Bluford Series novel in this book, alongside the true stories by teens. We hope you'll like it enough to continue reading. The more you read, the more you'll strengthen your reading skills. Teens at Youth Communication like the Bluford novels because they explore themes similar to those in their own stories. Your school may already have the Bluford books. If not, you can order them online for only $1.

Resources on the Web

We will occasionally post Think About It questions on our website, www.youthcomm.org, to accompany stories in this and other Youth Communication books. We try out the questions with teens and post the ones they like best. Many teens report that writing answers to those questions in a journal is very helpful.

How to Use This Book in Staff Training

Staff say that reading these stories gives them greater insight into what teens are thinking and feeling, and new strategies for working with them. You can help the staff you work with by using these stories as case studies.

Select one story to read in the group, and ask staff to identify and discuss the main issue facing the teen. There may be disagreement about this, based on the background and experience of staff. That is fine. One point of the exercise is that teens have complex lives and needs. Adults can probably be more effective if they don't focus too narrowly and can see several dimensions of their clients.

Ask staff: What issues or feelings does the story provoke in them? What kind of help do they think the teen wants? What interventions are likely to be most promising? Least effective? Why? How would you build trust with the teen writer? How have other adults failed the teen, and how might that affect his or her willingness to accept help? What other resources would be helpful to this teen, such as peer support, a mentor, counseling, family therapy, etc.

Resources on the Web

From time to time we will post Think About It questions on our website, www.youthcomm.org, to accompany stories in this and other Youth Communication books. We try out the questions with teens and post the ones that they find most effective. We'll also post lesson for some of the stories. Adults can use the questions and lessons in workshops.

Discussion Guide

Teachers and Staff:
How to Use This Book in Groups

When working with teens individually or in groups, using these stories can help young people face difficult issues in a way that feels safe to them. That's because talking about the issues in the stories usually feels safer to teens than talking about those same issues in their own lives. Addressing issues through the stories allows for some personal distance; they hit close to home, but not too close. Talking about them opens up a safe place for reflection. As teens gain confidence talking about the issues in the stories, they usually become more comfortable talking about those issues in their own lives.

Below are general questions that can help you lead discussions about the stories, which help teens and staff reflect on the issues in their own work and lives. In most cases you can read a story and conduct a discussion in one 45-minute session. Teens are usually happy to read the stories aloud, with each teen reading a paragraph or two. (Allow teens to pass if they don't want to read.) It takes 10-15 minutes to read a story straight through. However, it is often more effective to let workshop participants make comments and discuss the story as you go along. The workshop leader may even want to annotate her copy of the story beforehand with key questions.

If teens read the story ahead of time or silently, it's good to break the ice with a few questions that get everyone on the same page: Who is the main character? How old is she? What happened to her? How did she respond? Etc. Another good starting question is: "What stood out for you in the story?" Go around the room and let each person briefly mention one thing.

Then move on to open-ended questions, which encourage participants to think more deeply about what the writers were feeling, the choices they faced, and they actions they took. There are no right or wrong answers to the open-ended questions. Open-ended questions encourage participants to think about how the themes, emotions and choices in the stories relate to their own lives. Here are some examples of open-ended questions that we have found to be effective. You can use variations of these questions with almost any story in this book.

—What main problem or challenge did the writer face?

—What choices did the teen have in trying to deal with the problem?

—Which way of dealing with the problem was most effective for the teen? Why?

—What strengths, skills, or resources did the teen use to address the challenge?

—If you were in the writer's shoes, what would you have done?

—What could adults have done better to help this young person?

—What have you learned by reading this story that you didn't know before?

—What, if anything, will you do differently after reading this story?

—What surprised you in this story?

—Do you have a different view of this issue, or see a different way of dealing with it, after reading this story? Why or why not?

Credits

The stories in this book originally appeared in the following Youth Communication publications:

"Deciding My Own Worth," by Juelz Long, *New Youth Connections*, May/June 2006

"Sista on the Run (From the Past)," by Wunika Hicks, *Represent*, September/October 1993

"My Foster Mother Is My Best Friend," by Omar Sharif, *Represent*, November/December 1993

"Great Expectations," by Hattie Rice, *Represent*, July/August 2006

"Not What A Foster Parent Should Be," by Anonymous, *Represent*, November/December 1997

"She's Gay: And the Best Foster Mom I Know," by Arelis Rosario, *Represent*, January/February 2002

"Rewriting the Script," by Alex Withers, *New Youth Connections*, January/February 2008

"She's Not In It for the Money," by Jeffrey Allan Culbertson, *Represent*, March/April 1999

"Getting Hurt All Over Again," by Arelis Rosario, *Represent*, January/February 2002

"The Other Side of the Story," by Natasha Santos, *Represent*, July/August 2006

"A Foster Mother from Hell," by Angi Baptiste, *Represent*, March/April 1994

"I'm Not Safe Here," by Tamara Strectching, *Represent*, July/August 2008

"My Foster Mom Is Mad Cool," by Monique Martin, *Represent*, May/June 1998

"A Hi-Bye Relationship," by Cynthia Orbes, *Represent*, July/August 2006

"Why I'll Be a Foster Mother," by Tamara Ballard, *Represent*, March/April 1997

"My Place in the World," by Fannie Harris, *Represent*, November/December 2005

"Learning to Love Again," by Aquellah Mahdi, *Represent*, July/August 2006

"How to Get to Know a New Family," *Represent*, July/August 2006

"The First Good Christmas," by Aquellah Mahdi, *Represent*, November/December 2007

About
Youth Communication

Youth Communication, founded in 1980, is a nonprofit youth development program located in New York City whose mission is to teach writing, journalism, and leadership skills. The teenagers we train become writers for our websites and books and for two print magazines, *New Youth Connections*, a general-interest youth magazine, and *Represent*, a magazine by and for young people in foster care.

Each year, up to 100 young people participate in Youth Communication's school-year and summer journalism workshops where they work under the direction of full-time professional editors. Most are African American, Latino, or Asian, and many are recent immigrants. The opportunity to reach their peers with accurate portrayals of their lives and important self-help information motivates the young writers to create powerful stories.

Our goal is to run a strong youth development program in which teens produce high quality stories that inform and inspire their peers. Doing so requires us to be sensitive to the complicated lives and emotions of the teen participants while also providing an intellectually rigorous experience. We achieve that goal in the writing/teaching/editing relationship, which is the core of our program.

Our teaching and editorial process begins with discussions

between adult editors and the teen staff. In those meetings, the teens and the editors work together to identify the most important issues in the teens' lives and to figure out how those issues can be turned into stories that will resonate with teen readers.

Once story topics are chosen, students begin the process of crafting their stories. For a personal story, that means revisiting events in one's past to understand their significance for the future. For a commentary, it means developing a logical and persuasive point of view. For a reported story, it means gathering information through research and interviews. Students look inward and outward as they try to make sense of their experiences and the world around them and find the points of intersection between personal and social concerns. That process can take a few weeks or a few months. Stories frequently go through ten or more drafts as students work under the guidance of their editors, the way any professional writer does.

Many of the students who walk through our doors have uneven skills, as a result of poor education, living under extremely stressful conditions, or coming from homes where English is a second language. Yet, to complete their stories, students must successfully perform a wide range of activities, including writing and rewriting, reading, discussion, reflection, research, interviewing, and typing. They must work as members of a team and they must accept individual responsibility. They learn to provide constructive criticism, and to accept it. They engage in explorations of truthfulness, fairness, and accuracy. They meet deadlines. They must develop the audacity to believe that they have something important to say and the humility to recognize that saying it well is not a process of instant gratification. Rather, it usually requires a long, hard struggle through many discussions and much rewriting.

It would be impossible to teach these skills and dispositions as separate, disconnected topics, like grammar, ethics, or assertiveness. However, we find that students make rapid progress when they are learning skills in the context of an inquiry that is personally significant to them and that will benefit their peers.

When teens publish their stories—in *New Youth Connections* and *Represent,* on the web, and in other publications—they reach tens of thousands of teen and adult readers. Teachers, counselors, social workers, and other adults circulate the stories to young people in their classes and out-of-school youth programs. Adults tell us that teens in their programs—including many who are ordinarily resistant to reading—clamor for the stories. Teen readers report that the stories give them information they can't get anywhere else, and inspire them to reflect on their lives and open lines of communication with adults.

Writers usually participate in our program for one semester, though some stay much longer. Years later, many of them report that working here was a turning point in their lives—that it helped them acquire the confidence and skills that they needed for success in college and careers. Scores of our graduates have overcome tremendous obstacles to become journalists, writers, and novelists. They include National Book Award finalist Edwidge Danticat, novelist Ernesto Quinonez, writer Veronica Chambers and *New York Times* reporter Rachel Swarns. Hundreds more are working in law, business, and other careers. Many are teachers, principals, and youth workers, and several have started nonprofit youth programs themselves and work as mentors—helping another generation of young people develop their skills and find their voices.

Youth Communication is a nonprofit educational corporation. Contributions are gratefully accepted and are tax deductible to the fullest extent of the law.

To make a contribution, or for information about our publications and programs, including our catalog of over 100 books and curricula for hard-to-reach teens, see www.youthcomm.org

About The Editors

Al Desetta has been an editor of Youth Communication's two teen magazines, *Foster Care Youth United* (now known as *Represent*) and *New Youth Connections*. He was also an instructor in Youth Communication's juvenile prison writing program. In 1991, he became the organization's first director of teacher development, working with high school teachers to help them produce better writers and student publications.

Prior to working at Youth Communication, Desetta directed environmental education projects in New York City public high schools and worked as a reporter.

He has a master's degree in English literature from City College of the City University of New York and a bachelor's degree from the State University of New York at Binghamton, and he was a Revson Fellow at Columbia University for the 1990-91 academic year.

He is the editor of many books, including several other Youth Communication anthologies: *The Heart Knows Something Different: Teenage Voices from the Foster Care System*, *The Struggle to Be Strong*, and *The Courage to Be Yourself*. He is currently a freelance editor.

Keith Hefner co-founded Youth Communication in 1980 and has directed it ever since. He is the recipient of the Luther P. Jackson Education Award from the New York Association of Black Journalists and a MacArthur Fellowship. He was also a Revson Fellow at Columbia University.

Laura Longhine is the editorial director at Youth Communication. She edited *Represent*, Youth Communication's magazine by and for youth in foster care, for three years, and has written for a variety of publications. She has a BA in English from Tufts University and an MS in Journalism from Columbia University.

More Helpful Books
From Youth Comunication

 *Do You Have What It Takes? A Comprehensive Guide to Success After Foster Care.* In this survival manual, current and former foster teens show how they prepared not only for the practical challenges they've faced on the road to independence, but also the emotional ones. Worksheets and exercises help foster teens plan for their future. Activity pages at the end of each chapter help social workers, independent living instructors, and other leaders use the stories with individuals or in groups. (Youth Communication)

The Struggle to Be Strong: True Stories by Teens About Overcoming Tough Times. Foreword by Veronica Chambers. Help young people identify and build on their own strengths with 30 personal stories about resiliency. (Free Spirit)

 Depression, Anger, Sadness: Teens Write About Facing Difficult Emotions. Give teens the confidence they need to seek help when they need it. These teens write candidly about difficult emotional problems—such as depression, cutting, and domestic violence—and how they have tried to help themselves. (Youth Communication)

What Staff Need to Know: Teens Write About What Works. How can foster parents, group home staff, caseworkers, social workers, and teachers best help teens? These stories show how communication can be improved on both sides, and provide insight into what kinds of approaches and styles work best. (Youth Communication)

 *Out of the Shadows: Teens Write About Surviving Sexual Abuse.* Help teens feel less alone and more hopeful about overcoming the trauma of sexual abuse. This collection includes first-person accounts by male and female survivors grappling with fear, shame, and guilt. (Youth Communication)

Just the Two of Us: Teens Write About Building Good Relationships. Show teens how to make and maintain healthy relationships (and avoid bad ones). Many teens in care have had poor role models and are emotionally vulnerable. These stories demonstrate good and bad choices teens make in friendship and romance. (Youth Communication)

The Fury Inside: Teens Write About Anger. Help teens manage their anger. These writers show how they got better control of their emotions and sought the support of others. (Youth Communication)

Always on the Move: Teens Write About Changing Homes and Staff. Help teens feel less alone with these stories about how their peers have coped with the painful experience of frequent placement changes, and turnover among staff and social workers. (Youth Communication)

Two Moms in My Heart: Teens Write About the Adoption Option. Teens will appreciate these stories by peers who describe how complicated the adoption experience can be—even when it should give them a more stable home than foster care. (Youth Communication)

My Secret Addiction: Teens Write About Cutting. These true accounts of cutting, or self-mutilation, offer a window into the personal and family situations that lead to this secret habit, and show how teens can get the help they need. (Youth Communication)

Growing Up Together: Teens Write About Being Parents. Give teens a realistic view of the conflicts and burdens of parenthood with these stories from real teen parents. The stories also reveal how teens grew as individuals by struggling to become responsible parents. (Youth Communication)

To order these and other books, go to:
www.youthcomm.org
or call 212-279-0708 x115

CPSIA information can be obtained at www.ICGtesting.com

223980LV00006B/13/P